BEHIND THE IRON CURTAIN

A Teacher's Guide to East Germany and Cold War Activities

Jeffrey M. Byford

University Press of America,® Inc.
Lanham · Boulder · New York · Toronto · Plymouth, UK

Copyright © 2012 by
University Press of America,® Inc.
4501 Forbes Boulevard
Suite 200
Lanham, Maryland 20706
UPA Acquisitions Department (301) 459-3366

10 Thornbury Road
Plymouth PL6 7PP
United Kingdom

All rights reserved
Printed in the United States of America
British Library Cataloging in Publication Information Available

Library of Congress Control Number: 2012939175
ISBN: 978-0-7618-5932-1 (paperback : alk. paper)
eISBN: 978-0-7618-5933-8

♾™ The paper used in this publication meets the minimum
requirements of American National Standard for Information
Sciences—Permanence of Paper for Printed Library Materials,
ANSI Z39.48-1992

Contents

List of Tables	iv
List of Figures	v
Preface and Introduction	vi
Acknowledgments	vii
Chapter 1: Instruction and Planning	1
Chapter 2: The Making of the East German State	29
Chapter 3: The Enemy from Within: The Formation of the STASI	41
Chapter 4: The Berlin Wall: Divide and Rule	63
Chapter 5: Becoming a Good Socialist: Youth and Education	75
Chapter 6: The Planned Economy that Didn't have a Plan	81
Chapter 7: Life and Society in East Germany	97
Chapter 8: The Fall of East Germany	104
References	112
Index	114

LIST OF TABLES

Table 2.1: Characteristics of the Communist Political Economic System	31
Table 4.2: Selected Examples of Failed Escapes (1961–1989)	65
Table 5.1: Example of Organized Events for Jugendweihe	76
Table 5.2: Example of Education, Job Title, and Salary	77
Table 7.1: Olympic Medal Rankings of the German Democratic Republic	98
Table 7.2: Common Travel Destinations for East German Citizens	99
Table 7.3: Consumption of Selected Stimulates per East German	100
Table 8.1: Example of High Profile Trials of East German Officials	109

LIST OF FIGURES

Figure 2.1: General Structure of the Soviet/East German Government   32

Figure 3.1: Stasi Total Surveillance   44

Figure 6.1: Planning, Producing, and Distributing Goods   84

Figure 6.2: Issues Associated with Consumption and Manufacturing   86

Preface and Introduction

Arguably, one of the greatest challenges faced by social studies today is incorporating effective and interesting material and lessons into social studies curriculum while meeting all of the necessary requirements for local and state tests. This book was written to provide teachers, historians, curriculum directors, and students with an investigative insight of the Cold War from behind the Iron Curtain. Such a text is designed to provide practical strategies that may be used in a variety of social studies classrooms. Since most traditional classroom textbooks discuss a limited amount of Cold War events, and often from a Western/United States perspective.

Chapter 1, "Instruction and Planning," will provide readers with the "how to" in teaching the books activities with examples taken throughout the book.

Chapter 2, "The Making of the East German State," provides readers with detailed information on the creation of East Germany, political issues associated with a divided Germany, and growing pains associated with socialist reform. This chapter is ideal for teaching students in both United States and world history classrooms.

Chapter 3, "The Enemy from Within and State Security: The Formation of the Stasi," provides readers accounts dealing with the creation of the Ministry of State Security, which viewed themselves as "protectors of socialism." This chapter is ideal for teaching students in the United States history, world history, or current issues classrooms.

Chapter 4, "The Berlin Wall: Divide and Rule," provides readers with the East German political, social, and economic rationale for constructing the Berlin Wall. This chapter is ideal for teaching students in the United States history, world history, geography, or current issues classrooms.

Chapter 5, "Becoming a Good Socialist: Youth and Education," provides readers with a creative insight on how youth and government perceived both society and education behind the Iron Curtain. This chapter is ideal for teaching students in sociology and psychology classrooms.

Chapter 6, "The Planned Economy that Didn't have a Plan," provides readers with a simplistic approach to teaching socialism, communism, and the idea behind planned economies. In addition, this chapter provides insight on East German/Eastern Bloc consumerism and its inherited demise. This chapter is ideal for teaching students in United States history, world history, economics, government, sociology, or current issues classrooms.

Chapter 7, "Life and Society in East Germany," provides readers with a glimpse of daily life behind the Iron Curtain. Family structure, recreation and leisure, and religion are discussed. This chapter is ideal for teaching students in United States history, world history, current issues, sociology, economics, and psychology classrooms.

Chapter 8, "The Fall of East Germany," provides readers a timeline on the "how" and "why" East Germany began its spiral downward and the eventual opening of the Berlin Wall. This chapter is ideal for teaching students in the United States history, world history, current issues, and government classrooms.

Jeffrey M. Byford, Ph.D.
The University of Memphis, January 2012

ACKNOWLEDGMENTS

I would like to thank my wife, family, and friends for their love and support while writing this book. Without them, this wouldn't have been possible

ONE

INSTRUCTION AND PLANNING

INTRODUCTION

One of the most difficult tasks for social studies teachers is to provide interesting and informative lessons which lend themselves to a variety of learning styles in any given classroom. Often, time needed to design, plan for, and conduct such activities takes hours or days of valuable time and effort. Time needed to ensure various levels of Blooms taxonomy, measurable goals and objectives and required content can be overwhelming to both novice and veteran teachers. Research (Bonwell and Eison 1991; Chiodo and Byford 2004; Russell and Byford 2006; Wheeler 2006) suggests that students prefer instructional strategies that provide a variety of (differentiated) ways to learn and explore the content at hand and teachers who present such activities and lessons teach more effectively in terms of retention of content knowledge. D. Krathwohl (2002) suggests that students are more likely to become actively engaged in higher order learning such as analysis, synthesis, and evaluation when curriculum delivery methods vary in design. Such variation in lessons and activities encourage and create individual self-reflection in an effort to promote both individual and group problem-solving skills. Therefore, our goal as social studies teachers is to design curriculum that encourages critical thinking without the reliance of traditional direct instruction on a daily basis.

The goal of this book is twofold: (1) To provide the social studies teacher a variety of tested method procedures that may not be commonly used on a daily basis. The goal of such differentiated instructional procedures is to provide a foundation and rationale on how each procedure is structured and operates in the classroom environment. Such procedures are not solely intended for teaching about the Cold War but may be used to present additional historical topics or issues. (2) To provide teachers with additional supplemental material over the Cold War. The following eight chapters and lessons, which focus on East Germany, may be used in a variety of social studies disciplines to support traditional school systems–mandated material.

THE CASE STUDY APPROACH

The concept behind the case study method is to focus intensively on *limited* situations rather than on a large variety of sweeping events. The object with such an approach is the investigations of single institutions, decisions, situations, dilemmas, or individual actions. According to Kunselman and Johnson (2004), the perceived benefits for students who follow the case study method are that they aid (1) a better understanding of complicated issues, historical events, and materials; (2) discussion of issues with peers; and (3) engagement in informative discussions related to information presented. In terms of higher level learning, "the case study approach increases the possible use of Bloom's taxonomy by using analysis, evaluation, and conceptualizing, while identifying concepts, principles and issues within a given situation in relation to content" (87).

Naturally, the nature of case study materials may vary considerably. Generally, case studies are dependent upon discussion. The teacher plays a role in the case study approach. The inductive or discovery approach allows students to search for and reach conclusions on their own, rather than having the conclusion or knowledge given to them by the teacher. Within the inductive or discovery approach, there are two applications of delivery: the open-ended approach and the close-ended approach. The open-ended approach occurs when the teacher has not previously decided what knowledge or conclusions students are to gain for the study of a case. In this approach, the teacher is willing to entertain ideas, approaches, or suggestions given by students as long as such suggestions are serious and relevant.

Contrasting the open-ended approach, the closed-ended approach follows the assumption that the teacher has already determined the knowledge, structures, or conclusions that students will discover. In terms of varying degrees of subtlety, students are directed or prompted to reach the "correct" conclusion. Most social studies teachers encourage the open-ended approach due to increased freedom to ascertain more solutions, outcomes, and most importantly, no clear "right" answers.

The case study approach consists of four steps designed to introduce, distribute, develop, and reinforce in an effort to provide students with a snapshot of an era or time period. Such steps provide the teacher a script or order of events when conducting such a lesson. The following steps are required in developing the case study method procedure:

Step 1: Introduction
Step 2: Learning experience distributed
Step 3: Comprehension development
Step 4: Reinforcement/Extension

The following lesson is an example of the case study procedure. A more detailed example may be found in Chapter Three. This case study lesson investigates the activities of the Ministerium fur Staatssicherheit; Ministry for State

Security (Stasi) attempts to conduct both foreign and domestic espionage in an effort to protect the German Democratic Republic (GDR).

Case Study Example Lesson: The West German Spies Dilemma: A Case Study about Stasi Foreign and Domestic Espionage

For the Teacher: Teaching about the Cold War, specifically about tensions between the Eastern Bloc and Western Europe, may be difficult. This case study affords you the ability to use the case study strategy in an effort to illustrate the knowledge, resourcefulness, and creativity used by the East German Secret Police (Stasi) in an effort to maintain their "socialist utopian state." This lesson is designed to both broaden students' cooperative skills and increase their level of critical inquiry. In an effort to guide one through this lesson, steps are provided below.

Step 1: Introduction: In an effort to "set the stage" for this lesson, it is recommended students be placed into groups of three to four students. Inform the students the year is 1965 and they are spies working undercover in East Berlin. They have been working for the West German government for several years providing excellent information. However, your handler (the West German government) would like to have additional information on ALL aspects of the East German Secret Police (Stasi) and their abilities to gather secret information. You have received a "once in a lifetime opportunity." After following a Stasi agent for weeks, your team has stumbled onto some valuable information. You will only have *15 minutes* to investigate each of the documents. Your goal is for the Stasi agent not to discover that his documents have been compromised. Now, your team has to decide what is important. There are NO set criteria on what is considered valuable, so you must work as a team.

Step 2: Learning Experience Distributed: Provide each group with their instruction sheet document and ten documents. Each document deals with unique situations and operations conducted by Stasi agents both in East and West Germany. Information is diverse, much like most Stasi operations. Indicate to the class that they have a total of fifteen minutes to analyze, evaluate, and select the most valuable documents. The key issues are which are important and not important?

Step 3: Comprehension Development: Allow students to evaluate each document. Provide students with the information sheet. Students are to only select (photograph) the *three most important documents*. Students are also instructed to rank the importance of the remaining seven documents. It is important to understand there are no set criteria for the value of each document. Students are to determine the importance and *perceived* value by West German authorizes. Students are to defend their selections.

Step 4: Reinforcement/Extension: Ask each group to identify and explain their top three documents. After each group has completed their selections, inform students (through discussion or notes) how and why East Germany was so resourceful in its spying operations throughout the world and on its own people.

The West German Spies Dilemma

The date is 15 May 1965. For the past two years, you and your friends have secretly worked for the West German military by spying on the East Berlin's Ministerium fur Staatssicherheit (Stasi) headquarters and high ranking officials in the Socialist Unity Party (SED).

Your team has collected excellent information in the past, and recently, your information has been "noticed" by those at higher levels of the West German government. Your team has recently been tasked to follow several "medium level" Stasi agents whom you believe have a mix of interesting information regarding the West along with situations dealing with civil rights and espionage issues within East Germany. As your team follows one of your "identified" agents, you find the rare opportunity to "liberate" a briefcase when the Stasi agent is preoccupied. With briefcase in hand, your team makes a quick break to one of your predetermined safe houses.

Once the situation seems safe, you realize the importance of examining and selecting what you believe is the most important information to send back to West Berlin. You know it will not be long before the Stasi agent will reluctantly report the missing documents. Now, time is NOT on your side. Your employer (West Germany) needs good information on ALL aspects of East Germany. Your information can provide valuable information about this closed society. It is up to your team to decide what is important and what is not.

When you open the folder, you find ten documents dealing with a range of issues. Instead of sending all of the documents to your West German handler, you are only allowed to *take photographs* of what your team believes are the *three most important documents*. Remember, information is important and time is NOT on your side. It's only a matter of time before the Volkspolizei (police) will begin their search of each building. Now you must rank the importance of each document. You will be asked to justify your decision!

The three most important documents (high priority) to be sent to West Berlin with your film are:
1.
2.
3.

The three documents of importance (medium priority) that you would send if you had more film are:
1.
2.
3.

The five documents of low importance (low priority) that you would send if you had lots of extra film are:
 1.
 2.
 3.
 4.

Discussion Starters

How did your team decide on the importance of each document?
What did your team decide what is important: Military information or information on East German citizens?
In your opinion, which had greater value: information about civilians or government activity?

Case Study Sample Documents

TOP SECRET—Document #1
Date: 1 June 1964
Subject: West Berlin Interceptions
Acting on Order No: 2872 from Comrade Mielke, all high profile escapees from GDR soil are to captured and returned to the GDR or eliminated due to their high security risks of false propaganda against the State. West German youth organizations are of particular interest. The following names have been reported as collaborators against the GDR. Immediate action is requested.

Ruth von Stahl, age 29 years, student at Free Berlin University. Subject has provided "technical assistants" to various Western newspapers regarding Wall fortifications and detailed surveillance of border guard shift changes.

Mikel Dahl, age 24 years, "disk jockey" at Freedom Radio located in West Berlin. Subject has played music deemed "subversive" to the Socialist cause. Subject has on numerous occasions has directed East Berlin citizens to escape and rise up against the GDR.

Anna Ulm, age 20 years, waitress who negotiated border obstacles in 1961. Subject is currently active in raising funds to help East German citizens pay for their freedom.

TOP SECRET—Document #2
Suspicion: Terrorist Activities
Name: Hans Cole (Case #10092)
Date of Initial Observation: 10 April 1963
Charge: False Claims Against the GDR and Socialist Cause
Informant: Classified
Allegations to crime(s):
On 5 April 1963, Cole, a factory worker outside of East Berlin was identified after Cole's shift supervisor contact the Volkspolizie (police) after Hans repeatedly told peers about his willingness to "make a statement" against oppression. Agent XXXX interviewed the shift supervisor and began the initial observation of Cole on 10 April, 1963. While at work, Agents XXXX and XXXX successfully entered Cole's home. Black powder and what appear to be machined tubes with caps were found. Items were photographed and left.
On 14 April 1963, Hans told local priest at location XXXX that "The East Germans government would collapse at the hands of the people" and "the socialist cause and state was ruthless and paranoid in controlling the behavior of the masses." Initial audio recordings within XXXX church suggest that Cole is willing to enact harm to either Volkspolizie or Ministerium fur Staatssicherheit (Stasi) offices.

TOP SECRET—Document #3
Date: 23 September 1963
Subject: Karl Schmillberg (Case #22345)
Operation: Bavarian Homecoming
Karl Schmillberg is employed by the United States Army 427th Military Intelligence Battalion, West Berlin. As a civilian with special security clearances, Schmillberg has access to sensitive information.
On 19 September 1963, Schmillberg stole classified documents using a military mailbag. His escape was successful, using false documents prepared by Agent XXXX to enter East Berlin. The significance of Schmillberg's information is as follows:
- Names of forty-two American/West German agents working in East Germany.
- Codes to NATO forces scrambled communications (limited).
- American/West German agents monitoring rail yard/railroad operations pertaining to Russian tank transportation.
- Detailed railroad diagrams and communications from the Poland.

TOP SECRET—Document #4
Suspicion: Antigovernment propaganda
Name: Miriam Mundt (Case #00988)
Date of Initial Observation: 6 February 1963
Charge: Enemy of the State
Informant: Christopher Hans
Allegations to crime(s):
Miriam Mundt, age 18 years, was reported to Stasi officials for allegedly printing antigovernment propaganda against the GDR. On 28 January 1963, Mundt, along with a friend, made and distributed pamphlets to speak out against local party (Government) reforms. Subject allegedly pasted pamphlets at the main train station in Leipzig. Mundt, on 29 January, placed two pamphlets with Peter Hans, a former schoolmate. Christopher Hans, Peter's father and active member in the Solialistische Einheitspartei (East German Socialist Unity Party), turned the evidence in to Stasi station #325 in Leipzig. On 6 February, agents entered Mundt's residence and found rubber stamp letters that were similar in both font size and letters used on pamphlets.

Content-Centered Learning

Content-centered learning was developed by Stahl (1979) in an effort to stress the common elements that exist across various approaches to teaching values education. Three styles of content-centered lessons will be discussed: forced choice, rank-order, and classification. Regardless of the particular style of content-centered lesson, five characteristics of moral dilemmas are considered:

1. There is a neutral issue or context that people may react to or consider in terms of some values or moral belief (e.g., supporting the suppression of pro-democracy demonstrators in the name of socialism, or supporting "pro-Marxist rebels in Central America during the Cold War).
2. A value or moral issue that could be considered in its polar forms (good versus evil, Communism versus Capitalism, etc.).
3. A value or moral issue in conflict with another value or moral issue in a problem-solving situation (e.g., supporting religious rights versus government atheism, supporting human rights versus state/national security)
4. A value or moral issue that may cause conflict because it allows for two or more possible choices.
5. A situation where two or more values or moral issues are applicable and may conflict with one another.

Forced-Choice Format

The forced-choice format provides the students with a situation where a major *character* or *group* is forced to make a decision and the alternatives that are available to them are limited and are often viewed as being all good or all bad that the students may select from. In short, students are forced to choose and forced to choose from a *limited* number of options. At the same time, students must understand that to consider other options or to consider combining the alternatives is unacceptable. Therefore, students can pick only *one* option and defend their rationale for its selection. This approach (forced-choice) represents one type of decision-making situation that students face. Key elements required in a forced-choice lesson:

1. A situation (may be brief) where either a group or individual/character is forced to make a decision.
2. Various alternatives are provided. Students do not make their own choices.
3. There is a process of elimination: three possible choices and then *one* best choice.
4. Discussion starters given individually provided to the group or discussed by the teacher in an effort to take the moral dilemma(s) to additional levels.

The following example is of a forced-choice format designed to present an ethical dilemma regarding the border security of the Berlin Wall.

Forced-Choice Lesson Example: Heinrich Lummer—East German Border Guard

Heinrich Lummer was nineteen-years-old when he was told to enter the East German army "in an effort to serve the socialist agenda of the East German people." Raised in East Berlin, Heinrich privately hated the socialist government and "wall of oppression" between East and West Berlin. However, in fear of the government's harsh treatment of those who questioned the government and possible Stasi spies within his unit, he was reluctant to express his disgust. Assigned to the northern sector of the Berlin Wall, Heinrich regularly witnessed civilian brutality at the hands of East German border guards. One summer night while on patrol, Heinrich tossed a note in an empty bottle over the Wall to the West Berlin sector. In the note, Heinrich anonymously described in detail his hatred for the Wall, the socialist government and the Soviet Union's presence in East Germany. Three days later, a West German news radio station read Heinrich's anonymous letter to their Western audience in an effort to document the oppression of the East German people. Three weeks after the radio broadcast while working in his border guard unit's barracks, Heinrich, along with others were arrested by three Stasi agents. It was noted at his arrest that a Stasi spy working within the West Berlin radio station copied the note and through military records had traced the note to his unit. Heinrich and ten fellow border guards were charged with espionage and transported to the hated Brandenburg prison.

As a high ranking member of the East German secret police (Stasi), you must individually select one of the following actions. Please consider the nature of the crime against the East German people and how to prevent similar future situation found above.

1. Deprive Heinrich of food and water for an extended period of time until he confesses to crimes against the socialist state. Make him serve ten to fifteen years of hard labor.
2. Arrest Heinrich's family and charge them with "failure to report crimes against the State." Make an example of Heinrich's mother with a one year sentence of hard labor.
3. Reward the Stasi spy working at the West German news radio station with a promotion and increase incentives to expose border guards whom he *suspects* of antigovernment activities.
4. Isolate Heinrich's officer in charge of his unit until he gives a confession. Once a confession is made, execute him for treason against the people and not properly controlling his unit. Rotate guards on patrol each evening in an effort to promote distrust and fear to conduct such antigovernment activities.

5. Reassign all members of Heinrich's unit to remote locations throughout East Germany.
6. Force confessions from several of Heinrich's unit. Each confession will be followed by two years of hard labor.
7. Increase electronic surveillance of all guards patrolling the Berlin Wall.
8. Secretly assign Stasi agents to each border guard unit. All suspicious activity will be reported and *suspected* guards will be reassigned or jailed.
9. Imprison Heinrich for life, making an example to fellow border guard units of the harsh punishment for espionage activities against the East German people/state. Rotate guards on patrol each evening in an effort to promote distrust and fear to conduct such antigovernment activities.

In a group, you must agree on one of the above options offered. As a group, you should seek some basis for agreement. The group must make every attempt to reach a common conclusion to protect the Socialist State of East Germany. The three possible actions taken by the Stasi were narrowed down to:
1.
2.
3.

Of the three decisions listed above, the best is:

Discussion Starters
1. Is it correct for a government to spy on its own citizens? Try to give an example of when it's appropriate and when it's not appropriate.
2. Suppose you were in charge of the West Berlin radio station, would you have read the letter knowing there was a possibility of a Stasi crackdown?
3. Do you believe Heinrich's open questioning of his government's political policies and his actions is espionage?

Rank-Order Format

The rank-order format provides the student with a situation where a major character or group is forced to make a decision and where alternatives available are provided. This format makes students consider the relative value of a number of options to one another such that they assign a specific rank order to each option while considered both potential positive and negative consequences. Key elements required in a rank-order lesson are:

1. A situation where a group or character/individual is placed into a situation.
2. Students are given "deciding factors," in which students decide which options are most important and which options are least important. *These options are based on information found within the dilemma.* Provide several options.
3. An individual decision chart used to "rank" options along with positive/negative consequences for each.
4. Students are given "personal actions" that can be considered acts carried out by the student to help solve the situation at-hand. Provide several options. (Optional)
5. An individual decision chart used to "rank" options along with positive/negative consequences for each. (Optional)

The following example is of a rank-order format designed to present an ethical dilemma regarding the border security of the Berlin Wall.

Rank-Order Lesson Example: Heinrich Lummer—East German Border Guard

Heinrich Lummer was nineteen-years-old when he was told to enter the East German army "in an effort to serve the socialist agenda of the East German people." Raised in East Berlin, Heinrich privately hated the socialist government and "wall of oppression" between East and West Berlin. However, in fear of the government's harsh treatment of those who questioned the government and possible Stasi spies within his unit, he was reluctant to express his disgust. Assigned to the northern sector of the Berlin wall, Heinrich regularly witnessed civilian brutality at the hands of East German border guards. One summer night while on patrol, Heinrich tossed a note in an empty bottle over the wall to the West Berlin sector. In the note, Heinrich anonymously described in detail his hatred for the Wall, the socialist government, and the Soviet Union's presence in East Germany. Three days later a West German news radio station read Heinrich's anonymous letter to their Western audience in an effort to document the oppression of the East German people. Three weeks after the radio broadcast, while working in his border guard unit's barracks, Heinrich, along with others, was arrested by three Stasi agents. It was noted at his arrest that a Stasi spy, working within the West Berlin radio station, copied the note and through military records, had traced the note to his unit. Heinrich and ten fellow border guards were charged with espionage and transported to the hated Brandenburg prison.

As a high ranking member of the East German secret police (Stasi), you must explore the following actions/options. Please consider the nature of the crime against the East German people and how to prevent similar future situation found above.

1. Deprive Heinrich of food, water, and sleep for an extended period of time until he confesses to crimes against the socialist state.
2. Arrest Heinrich's family and charge them with "failure to report crimes against the State." Make an example of Heinrich's mother with a one year sentence of hard labor.
3. Reward the Stasi spy working at the West German news radio station with a promotion and increase incentives to expose border guards who he *suspects* of antigovernment activities.
4. Isolate Heinrich's officer in charge of his unit until he gives a confession. Once a confession is made, deport him for treason against the people and not properly controlling his unit. Rotate guards on patrol each evening in an effort to promote distrust and fear to conduct such antigovernment activities.
5. Reassign all members of Heinrich's unit to remote locations throughout East Germany.
6. Force confessions from several of Heinrich's unit. Each confession will be followed by two years of hard labor.
7. Increase electronic surveillance of all guards patrolling the Berlin Wall.
8. Secretly assign Stasi agents to each border guard unit. All suspicious activity will be reported and *suspected* guards will be reassigned or jailed.
9. Kidnap the West Berlin DJ who read the letter to his audience and smuggle him to East Berlin to stand trial.

After evaluating the above options, rank in order the most to least acceptable action/option to be taken. Whether individually or in a group, make every attempt to reach a common conclusion to protect the Socialist State of East Germany.

Decision Sheet:

(How would you rank your options?) **Assigned Rank of Most Acceptable**	**Option Number**	**Positive/Negative Outcome**
	Deprivation of food, water, and sleep	
	Arrest of family	
	Reward Stasi spy	
	Deportation of commanding officer	
	Reassign unit	
	Confession with hard labor for unit members	
	Increase surveillance	
	Stasi to border	
	Kidnap West Berliner	

Discussion Starters
1. Is it correct for a government to spy on its own citizens? Try to give an example of when it's appropriate and when it's not appropriate.
2. Suppose you were in charge of the West Berlin radio station; would you have read the letter knowing there was a possibility of a Stasi crackdown?

Classification Format

The classification format provides the student with a situation where a major character or group is forced to make a decision and where alternatives available are provided. However, in this format, the person or group is forced to divide the alternatives into three broad categories or classes (i.e., alternatives most wanted to keep, alternatives least wanted to keep, and those that fit neither set of alternatives listed). Thus, the person or group is forced into a *compromising* or *bargaining* position in which they might identify what they want to hold and what they are willing to give up to preserve or protect something else. This, in essence, develops the compromise and consensus skills necessary in everyday life situations. Key elements required in a classification lesson are:

1. A dilemma faced by a student or group.
2. A list of alternatives available. More alternatives give students a better selection and provide more depth to the lesson.
3. An area for students to list the *three* (or different amount) best alternatives/policies with a rationale.
4. An area to divide the student/groups alternatives into three categories: most likely to work, least likely to work, and alternative fit neither. You will notice this lesson has three required alternatives. This is flexible. Please have at least two required responses.

The following lesson is designed using the principles of the classification format. The following lesson provides students with various methods to attempt to escape to West Berlin.

Classification Lesson Example: Escape from East Berlin

The date is 15 May 1964. You and your friends are citizens in the German Democratic Republic (East Germany). However, there is nothing "democratic" about the oppressive communist government. Since your country's birth in 1949 from Russian occupation, your government has become increasing paranoid about its labor force leaving for the West. The Berlin Wall has significantly reduced your fellow East Germans from traveling to West Berlin. The East German secret police (Stasi) are not only ruthless in spying on the citizens of East Germany but also in how they "obtain" information. Stasi infiltration into every aspect of East German life is guaranteed.

The communist "planned economy" in which you live is marginal at best compared to your fellow Germans living in West Berlin. Often, when you and your friends walk beside the fortified wall separating the two cities, you can hear and see the fast-paced lifestyles of West Berlin. This sense of freedom, along with recent arrests of several friends by the Stasi, has only fueled your desires to escape to a better life. With this desire also comes fear. Since the wall's initial construction in 1961, over thirty East Germans have died trying to escape. It has been rumored that some have escaped while others who are caught simple disappear. Successfully escaping is a good thing, but it will come with consequences. When and if you and your friends escape to West Berlin, the Stasi and other government officials will act swiftly when you fail to report to your assigned jobs the following day. Most likely, your family will be arrested along with friends not directly associated with your escape.

Earlier this morning, you had a brief opportunity to "peek" at a folder with top secret Stasi documents. Consider this a rare gift. The Stasi agent who carelessly left this material unattended will pay for his mistakes later. State police are aware of the situation but do not know if anyone has actually examined the documents. Later that evening, you and your friends sit down in your apartment to discuss the following possible escape scenarios:

1. With scrap metal and a motorcycle engine, build a small ultra light–styled aircraft. Practice will not be possible, so mark your aircraft with Russian markings. It is believed that a GDR border guard will fire upon a Soviet aircraft.
2. Using sewage access covers (manholes), you could attempt to escape through the elaborate sewage system that connects West Berlin. At designated "choke" points throughout the sewage system are welded bars similar to those found in prisons.
3. Build a hot air balloon from scrap parts and by piecing together bits of nylon and bed sheets to make a frighteningly fragile escape. Gas burners from your apartments will act as engines.
4. Steal a Russian-built, East German armored vehicle and drive it into the Wall.
5. Drive a stolen delivery truck at full speed into wall fortifications, and then attempt to climb the electric fence using deflated rubber inner tubes.
6. Use an inflatable mattress and attempt to swim one of the canals or rivers at night in an attempt to avoid East German patrols.
7. Attempt to gather materials and make (as close as possible) East German border guard uniforms. Making correct identification papers will be almost impossible. Take a GDR soldier hostage and attempt to escape through one of the eight checkpoints with West Berlin.
8. Steal a State-owned bus and attempt to smash it into wall fortifications, and then attempt to climb the electric fence using deflated rubber inner tubes.
9. Dig a tunnel to escape. Water tables (amount of water found in the soil) are generally high. Because of this, GDR border guards sporadically check buildings and ground for tunneling activities.
10. Other: Your group develops a plan of escape.

Instead of trying all of the above, your group of friends believes that some escape scenarios have better chances of success than others. With this in mind, your group must pick the one best plan to escape.

The most realistic and best plan for escape is:
   1.

Three other plans that might work (according to your groups ranking) are:
   2.
   3.
   4.

The remaining plans that are least likely to work (according to your groups ranking) are:
   5.
   6.
   7.
   8.
   9.
   10.

SIMULATIONS

As a former social studies teacher, I always enjoyed using simulations in my classes. Often, they brought excitement to the classroom and a sense of freedom from the day-to-day operations of lecture and other forms of instruction. Simulations are important to use in the social studies classroom because they allow students to perform as closely as they would in real-world situations. In effect, students gain knowledge and learn problem-solving skills while enacting events, situations, or decisions faced throughout history. In addition to the benefits of students enacting or performing replicated events in history, simulations increase the chances of learning more abstract concepts (Mills and Durden 1992; Slavin 1994). Furthermore, according to Driscoll (2005), simulations encourage students to:
1. Have a deeper level of insight;
2. Become more active in the learning process;
3. Retain knowledge and information longer than traditional (direct instruction) methods of instruction;
4. Develop both critical and analytical skills;
5. Sharpen speaking, presentation, and interaction skills.

While there are numerous ways to conduct a simulation, the following three components have been found useful.

Step 1: Teacher Instructions
   A. Briefly state the general (nonmeasurable) goal you wish for students to achieve from the activity.
   B. Measurable objectives (in either bullet or sentence form) describing measurable outcomes you wish for students to achieve.

Step 2: Procedure
   A. Step-by-step instructions for both the teacher and students presented sequentially to ensure all areas are presented and covered.
   B. Examples of previous works to demonstrate desired outcomes (optional).

Step 3: Assessment
   A. Scoring rubric to provide clear expectations in terms of product and assessment.

The following simulation is designed for students to escape East Berlin. This simulation evolved over the years from a quick fifteen-minute brainstorming activity into a complex, week-long assignment assessing students' linguistic, spatial, bodily-kinesthetic, logical-mathematical, and personal intelligences.

Simulation Lesson Example: Escape from Berlin

Goals: Given a simulation designed to provide students with insights into the working of a totalitarian society and the ruthless and oppressive brutality of a police state, this simulation is designed for students to better understand the difficulties involved in escaping from East Berlin through air, ground, or water.

Objectives: Given the opportunity, students will be able to:
1. Investigate documented escape attempts.
2. Analyze various methods of escape via water, air, and ground.
3. Construct a detailed escape plan.
4. Present escape plan to class.

Procedure: Teacher
1. Before one begins the "Escape from Berlin" activity, attempt to decorate the room in East German and Soviet flags and posters made by students. Nuclear survival guides, propaganda posters and pictures of the period, and historical readings and/or lectures are helpful in terms of background information.
2. Decide how you will divide student into teams. Before groups are formed, predetermine particular students that will act as Stasi agents and provide you with valuable escape attempt information. These students' identity status will remain secret.
3. Once students have either been placed into groups or allowed to select their own (preferred), provide each group with the simulation instructions for students and grading rubric. Carefully go through each document and check for understanding.

Procedure: Students
1. Once your group has been organized, carefully review the project guidelines and scoring criteria. After doing so, each student within the group should select a job title from a list developed by your teacher.
2. Once you begin to design an escape plan, your group may purchase hard-to-find items through the black market (your teacher). Your teacher will determine the amount of money each group will receive. Purchasing difficult to find items will allow your group the opportunity to discuss your escape plan with the teacher, who will remain neutral throughout the simulation.
3. In an effort to make the possibility of obtaining hard-to-find items, your teacher will determine given material through a coin toss. If the coin toss ruled against the purchase of the required goods, the group will have to abandon their plan.
4. The Stasi or East German Secret Police will also be present. It is recommended that you keep your plans a secret. If you hear other groups' plans, you may become an Unofficial Informer (IM) for the teacher.

5. You are NOT allowed to provide information on your OWN group.
6. You will make a detailed presentation of your escape plan to your peers. After all presentations, groups will then vote on the most realistic and probable plan of escape. Groups are not allowed to vote for their own escape plan.

Escape from East Berlin—Student Handout/Instructions

Time warp! You wake up to find that your group has been transformed into East Germans trapped behind the Berlin Wall in the year 1987. Your four to five member groups must escape. Your first step is organization. Security is critical. There are undercover members of the Stasi or secret police in this room. They will be rewarded if they "spy" on your escape plans. No person in your group can inform on your own group, but assume that other groups have Stasi in them. Your group will need to fill the following escape plan positions:

A. You will need to elect a *coordinator*. For security, this is the sole person who can talk to other groups or contact the black market.
B. A *researcher* is critical. Map-reading and ability to successfully tap into correct computer databases is vital. There can be more than one researcher in a group.
C. *Readers* must be present for the group presentation to the class. They must also read out the agreed answers to the coordinated plan. All members of your resistance group can help the reader answer questions during the presentation.
D. *Writers* must have either sufficient typing skills or legible handwriting and the ability to transcribe verbal information with accuracy. The ability to draw of draft plans can be a plus.

Your group must come up with an example of each of the three methods of escape. There are *over*, *under*, and *through*. You need to *concentrate on the pan that you decide to use*. You must *briefly mention* the two categories of escape methods that your group contemplated but didn't select. Diagrams, maps, and handouts should be used.

Security is paramount! Here, it can impact your grade. In reality, you could be sent to jail or be barred from higher education or a respectable job. Each time you talk to the black market, you must have a written record of our escape needs on your black market contact sheet. Turn in the sheet attached to your plan.

Your teacher is a neutral figure in this simulation. He/she is also someone your group can call upon for advice without fear of compromised security. They will tell you what can be purchased on black market versus what you can legally obtain on the open market. Any materials that need to be purchased on the black market are decided on a coin toss. If you lose the toss, you forfeit that particular plan and must design another. If you lose *four* coin tosses, your group will receive your first initial choice.

The black marketer is an illegal but somewhat tolerated part of the planned economy. The Volkspolizei (police) probably know who the person is, so expect them to take no chances on your behalf. Your coin toss simulates the reality the marketer might turn you in to stay in the good graces of the authorities. Their life is on the line even if your group is successful. Attempt to purchase weapons and the black marketer will turn you in!

Remember that by escaping, you will put your family in danger. They, most likely, will be punished, and you will surely never see them as long as the communist government remains in power.

Grading Rubric for Students

	Points
Written Grading Guide	
1st plan you didn't use and why. Length: One paragraph.	10
2nd plan you didn't use and why. Length: One paragraph.	10
3rd plan in detail. Length: Two pages minimum.	40
Security not broken. (Stasi agents obtain information.)	10
Black market paperwork.	10
Quality of writing (punctuation, grammar, etc.)	20
Verbal Grading Guide	
1st plan you didn't use and why. Length: One minute.	10
2nd plan you didn't use and why. Length: One minute.	10
3rd plan in detail. Length: Five to eight minutes.	40
Security not broken (Stasi agents informing class of plans.)	15
Answering questions from audience.	10
Visual aids.	10
Coordination of group effort.	5
Total	**200**

10-point security bonus for turning in <u>accurate</u> written plans of other groups.

PERSISTING ISSUES

Throughout social studies curriculum, one will find "persisting issues." Persisting issues are intended for students to be more than a spectator of curriculum, but to become thinking, acting, and evaluating participants in both social studies content and in modern life. Persisting issues do not provide students with traditional ready-made right or wrong answers to social issues and problems. Rather, the rationale behind persisting issues is for students to analyze situations for conflicting views and determine what they perceive as the correct outcome in an effort to relate historical events with students' individual perspectives. Research conducted by VanSledright (2004) indicated such active learning and student involvement aids in the connection of historical comprehension because "the common preoccupation with having students commit one fact after another to memory based on historical textbook recitations and lecture does little to build capacity to think historically" (233).

Generally, a "persisting issue" relates to the story or material related toward the textbook and is often considered a stand-alone lesson in terms on reliance from outside resources. Research (Hoagland 2000; Byford and Russell 2006) suggests the close relation with value dilemmas and the increased emphasis on student decision-making on problems presented and often connect the content to the individual interests of the students, thus increasing student interest in the content presented, and as a result, encouraging active engagement in the historical learning process. The major difference between the case study approach and persisting issues is the varying lack of structure in terms of prescribed steps found in both the case study approach and content-centered learning, while still placing students into value dilemmas.

The following persisting issues examples deal with the East German government's resentment of the Protestant Church and the recruitment process of IMs to gain information on East German citizens.

Persisting Issues Lesson Example: Operation Torch Light: East Germany's Policy of the Protestant Church

Directions: Read the following paragraph. As a high ranking member of the East German Ministry for State Security (MfS), it's your responsibility to evaluate the following report.

TOP SECRET
Date: 27 October 1988
Subject: Church activities
Operation: Torch light

Churches and religious communities in East Germany (GDR) were considered a thorn in the flesh of our country's Socialist Unity Party's control against Western influences and increased human rights complaints. With the initial conception of our country in 1949, churches have maintained a certain degree of independence. Many churches throughout the GDR have influenced their local towns in terms of actively criticizing government policy and maintaining a safe harbor for environmental, peace, and human rights groups. In addition, the Church is considered an active threat to the East Germany because the Church is viewed (1) as a strength in retreat (daily living) for East Germans, (2) as believing in an afterlife, (3) for its ability to connect with the masses through outside activities not connected to Church operations, and (4) as something that provides a competing set of values other than Communism. Therefore, the government's policy toward these groups is aimed to stop or at least decrease their influences by means of open or silent repression in the name of national security. Official MfS recommendations include the following actions:

1. Infiltrate Church seminaries (schools) to recruit IMs to provide future information on both fellow clergy and members.
2. Begin a campaign to squeeze out any form of religious education in schools and increase the pressure to conform to government policy through school-based campaigns.
3. Pressure younger generations to become more active in government-led activities (e.g., German Youth) and over time (years), the process of withering away Church support will drop to acceptable levels.
4. Create differences between East German youth and older generations on their views of the Church.
5. Spread misinformation (lies) about pastors from various churches in an effort to effectively turn against one another and Church policy.
6. Pressure pastors to become politically loyal to the socialist cause, and promise them, in return, concessions (breaks) to define the Church cause and directions.
7. Use blackmail (false information) to pressure selected pastors to step down.
8. Block acceptance to higher education, or expel students who either are not active in the Free German Youth (club for young socialists) or dedicated Socialist party members.
9. Require all youth to be confirmed members of the *Jugendweihe* (a socialist, atheist ritual) that represents loyalty to the socialist government.

As a high ranking member of the MfS, please answer the following questions. Be prepared to defend your decisions.
1. Which two proposed actions do you believe are most effective in decreasing the growing Church influence? Why?
2. Which two proposed actions do you believe are most unrealistic and least effective in controlling the Church's influence?
3. When, if ever, does the government have the right to control or influence organizations that directly influences its citizens? Are there exceptions?
4. Of the potential concerns expressed by the East German government about Church threats, which do you believe is most harmful? Least harmful?

Persisting Issues Lesson Example: How I Became an IM (Unofficial Informer)

Directions: Below is the case of a high school student living in East Germany who was approached and recruited to become an "unofficial informer." Read this short story. After doing so, decide if this student, in your opinion, took the appropriate action.

One day in April 1986, my school principal had me sent to the office. At first, I panicked, wondering what I had done. Was it skipping class, not doing my homework, or even smoking? In fact, I wasn't in trouble at all. My school principal wanted to introduce me to Mr. B. Once my principal made the formal introduction, he left. At first I thought Mr. B was a mechanic who had slipped into a suit; he had a small, chubby face and hands indicating that he worked outside and used them often. He appeared young, but I could tell he had been out of school for some time. He said he wanted to talk to me about several of the students in our school. At first I thought he might be in some leadership role with the Free German Youth Organization, but he didn't fit the image. He said he knew I was popular among different students and knew everybody well. He admitted that he knew little about the students because nobody would talk to him since he was an adult. In an effort to locate students who were "different," he was hoping to have private conversations with individual students like myself on a regular basis. It was a strange situation. He asked about certain students—what they did after school and more importantly, what they talked about when they attended church. What could I tell Mr. B that he didn't already know? How should I help him? Do I lie about students to him? At the end of our conversation, he told me he worked for the Ministry for State Security (Stasi) and that regardless of my decision, I couldn't tell anyone of our conversation, not even my parents. After Mr. B left, I became upset. Everyone knew who and what the Stasi did. The Stasi was a part of everyday life, much like family, school, church, etc.

Part of me was scared to talk to the Stasi, and the other part of me was curious and in a weird way, honored that they had come to me for information. Before I decided to "inform on others," I was required to write a declaration of commitment as an unofficial informer before I could receive any money for information. My declaration of commitment was the following:

I, _____, resident in Mitte, German Democratic Republic, voluntarily pledge to cooperate with Mfs (Stasi). I am prepared to report to the MfS in written and oral form about all things aimed against the security of the State. I will maintain absolute secrecy regarding this pledge towards all individuals. I have been instructed that violation of this pledge can cause harm to East Germany and I can be punished (for doing so). To preserve secrecy, I select the name Walter Uhlm.

Mr. B and I met regularly. I provided him information about students who often spoke negatively about the government. Mr. B appreciated the information and often told me how I was helping to protect the country from traitors and Western influences. Regardless of the information I provided, Mr. B regularly asked about what my friends did and when they attended church. He wanted to know if any of the students were being influenced by church members or the clergy and about the readings that were given to us. I was beginning to have questions about why Mr. B was so interested in youth activities at church. The only thing I knew was that I particularly liked the pastor at our local church. I didn't want to tell Mr. B anything about the people, the pastor, or his wife that would get them in trouble.

After reading the story, what would you do?
1. Would you agree with the student's decision to become an IM and provide potentially valuable information about friends and others? Why?
2. Suppose the school's principal asked for this information rather than Mr. B. Would this make a difference?
3. When is it okay to provide information about others? Why?
4. What do you believe are the reasons the student provided information?
5. Is it ever okay for the government to gather information on others? Why?

THE INQUIRY PROCESS

The term "inquiry" can be explained as searching for information by asking questions and examining things, which results in knowledge. The goal of inquiry-based teaching should teach students how to handle various forms of knowledge found in society by equipping students to discover *new knowledge* and *incorporate* that knowledge into their daily lives. In order to achieve this, students must formulate responses and answers through the use of sources. Such sources may be primary material, charts, graphs, photographs, movies, etc. The objective of inquiry is the *process*. Often the end product is less important but rather *how* the student developed their decision. You, the social studies teacher, play a *supportive* role. The five important characteristics of the inquiry approach are:
1. Focus is on the student.
2. Pace of instruction is *flexible* not *fixed*.
3. Students search for implications.
4. Students are encouraged to find *multiple* solutions.
5. Students must *justify* their responses.

The most common forms of inquiry are:
1. Inductive inquiry (small focus on topic to a larger focus on topic).
2. Deductive inquiry (large focus on topic to a smaller focus on topic).
3. Reflective inquiry (forming a hypothesis, gathering data from sources, and defending a decision).

The inquiry approach consists of six different models designed to provide a variety of both inductive and deductive approaches towards investigation. As in the case of the case study approach, each model consists of various steps designed to introduce, distribute, develop, and reinforce in an effort to provide students with a snapshot of an era or time period. Such steps provide the teacher with a script or order of events when conducting such a lesson. The following inquiry models and steps are provided below:

Model No. 1 (Inductive)
    Step 1: A question is raised and stated clearly.
    Step 2: A tentative answer is developed.
    Step 3: Evidence bearing on the tentative answer is gathered.
    Step 4: A conclusion is drawn from the evidence.
    Step 5: A conclusion is applied to the original question(s).

Model No. 2 (Inductive)
    Step 1: A question is raised.
    Step 2: Evidence is sought and evaluated.
    Step 3: A proposition or general rule is inferred from evidence.
    Step 4: A question is tested against the proposition or rule.

Step 5: In future situations, the proposition or rule is tested against new evidence.

Model No. 3 (Deductive)
    Step 1: A question is raised.
    Step 2: A known general rule is stated.
    Step 3: An answer is inferred from the general rule.
    Step 4: Evidence of the accuracy of the answer is sought.
    Step 5: Evidence is used to confirm the answer and general rule.

Model No. 4 (Historian's Model)
    Step 1: A question is raised.
    Step 2: The source is researched.
    Step 3: Evidence is interpreted.
    Step 4: Findings are presented.

Model No. 5 (Problem Solving)
    Step 1: Present a feeling of confusion or doubt to students.
    Step 2: Students recognize and define problems.
    Step 3: Analyze the problem and formulate hypotheses.
    Step 4: Gather evidence.
    Step 5: Verify and interpret evidence.
    Step 6: Formulate and accept conclusion.
    Step 7: Apply conclusions to topic.

Model No. 6 (Survey Research—Inductive)
    Step 1: Pose a problem.
    Step 2: Construct a hypothesis.
    Step 3: Construct sample pool and conduct survey.
    Step 4: Draw conclusion and report conclusion.

The following lesson is an example of the Model No. 1 procedure only. A more detailed example may be found in Chapter Two. This inquiry lesson asks students to investigate and incorporate material provided discussing the East German model of communism instituted at a local school level for investigative purposes only.

Inquiry Lesson Example: The (_____) Democratic Republic: An Inquiry Lesson about the use of Communist Political Model

For the Teacher:
In a world of various competing models of government, most students find the actual inner-workings to be difficult, at best, to understand. This lesson is designed to provide students with an insight on how, *in theory*, the communist model might be implemented at a personal level. Using pre-existing organizations, roles, and policies already established in your school, this lesson asks the students to take such established roles and create, *in theory*, a small communist model. The desired goal for this lesson is not to necessarily endorse or create an actual working communist model of government, but rather *personalize* such a model on a level students might better understand.

Step 1: A question is raised and stated clearly.
Ask the class what type of government their school models. Does their school have a student council or government? Are all groups, organizations, and students fairly represented? Would a better or different model of student government work?

Step 2: A tentative answer is developed.
Encourage a class discussion on the strengths and weakness of their school's current structure. Oddly enough, most schools have what is known as a "student council" which in fact is not a council but rather a loose interpretation of government. Ask students (either in small groups or as a class) if they believe the East German model of government *could* or *would* work at their school? What would they perceive as the potential strengths or weaknesses?

Step 3: Evidence bearing on the tentative answer is gathered.
Either in small groups or individually, provide students with the handout titled, "The Basic Structure of the East German Government" and any additional notes given in class or readings. Ask students to brainstorm of all the social clubs, organizations, and student representation at their school. After doing so, ask the students to insert such organizations based on the models provided.

Step 4: A conclusion is drawn from the evidence.
Have students or groups present their individual model to the class. Ask the students to discuss their diagrams and the possible strengths and weaknesses found within.

Step 5: Conclusion is applied to the original question.
On the board, have the class discuss and illustrate the overall strengths and weaknesses of using the East German model at their school.

TWO

THE MAKING OF THE EAST GERMAN STATE

It can be said that the German Democratic Republic (GDR) or East Germany was a direct creation and product of the Cold War. Created from the Soviet Union's occupied zone of Nazi Germany after World War II, the GDR was considered the "crown jewel" of all the occupied nations by the Soviet Union. Largely known and condemned throughout the world for its development and maintained enforcement of the Berlin Wall, the GDR was considered the model communist nation both economically and socially, ultimately becoming the second largest economy in the Eastern Bloc and the twelfth largest economy in the world (Jeffries and Melzer 1987). However, unlike its fellow communist nations, the GDR shared a common language, religion, and culture with its capitalist neighbor, West Germany. This unique relationship with the "class enemy," eventual financial failures, and growing antigovernment movements within communist nations eventually led to the collapse of East Germany's "communist utopia" and the reunification of East and West Germany in October 1990.

POST-WAR TRANSFORMATION OF SOCIETY

The beginning of what was known as the GDR has its origins at the 1945 Yalta Conference. Here, the allied powers of the United States, Soviet Union, England, and France agreed to separate Germany into four zones of occupation. With the total defeat of German forces inevitable, long-time German communist hiding in the Soviet Union began to return to Germany with the hope of establishing a communist state. Erich Mielke, a devout communist who fought against fascism in both Germany and Spain for fourteen years, returned to his native country to aid in the establishment of a Soviet puppet-communist state. Under the leadership and direction of Soviet General Marshal Zhukov, the Supreme Commander of Soviet forces in Germany and the leader of the Soviet Military Administration (SMA), the first "antifascist" political parties were formed: the German Communist Party and the German Socialist Party (Koehler 1999).

Initially, in the years immediately after the war, German citizens living in the occupied Russian zone rejected early attempts to confiscate and redistribute land. Because the Russians had suffered greatly at the hands of German forces within the Soviet Union, Russian forces and government officials were particularly brutal on the German population and cannibalized all of its remaining resources. Money, factories, food crops, and even railroads were disassembled and shipped back to the Soviet Union. Furthermore, throughout 1945 and 1946, German citizens living in the Soviet occupation zone endured arrests of suspected Nazi supporters, anticommunists, and critics of Soviet politics were arrested under the "de-Nazification" of Eastern Germany. Mielke, along with the Soviet Secret Police, performed this task with detailed precision. In fact, the numbers of "accused citizens" were so great, the Russians were forced to reopen two former Nazi death camps in Buchenwald and Sachsenhausen to hold suspected "enemies of the state" (Koehler 1999).

THE POWER ELITE:
THE CONCEPTION OF THE SOCIALIST UNITY PARTY

In the spring of 1946, the SMA ordered the Germany Communist Party and the German Socialist Party to put aside their resentment toward one another and unify to become the Socialist Unity Party (SED) in an effort to form a united front for a more politically stable East Germany operating under the communist political and economic model (see Table 2.1).

The task of essentially rebuilding East Germany's political system was left to a small core of East German communists with the financial and military support of the Soviet Union. Throughout a period of three years, this small core of communists traveled the country finding like-minded Germans who placed the SED as the leading and most influential authority when the German Democratic Republic was officially formed on the 7th of October 1949. The newly formed government's national flag consisted of three symbols representing the nation's population: the hammer (representing the workers), the compass (denoting the educated), and a wreath of wheat ears (standing for farmers), all embraced by a black, red, and yellow band or traditional German colors (Fritz 2009).

Despite some initial misgivings by a minority of East Germans, the SED became the leading political party and dominant political organization in East Germany. In an effort to appease the concerns of a single, dominant political party, the SED opened the East German Parliament (Volkskammer) or commonly referred to as the Party Congress to various political parties associated with communism.

The newly formed communist government of East Germany was appealing by many. The SED had two distinct advantages that helped it maintain control. First, Erich Honecker, a communist, along with the leadership of the SED, government officials were viewed as heroes who spent much of their lives on the run from or imprisoned by the Nazis. A clear break both ideologically and politically from the Nazi Germany past in 1949 appealed to most East Germans. This was the case particularly among the nation's youth who viewed communism as the answer to a world without wars, fairness, and equality, and most importantly, a society free from the exploitation of capitalism and money. In order to maintain this vision, the Socialist Unity Party needed to retrain East Germans to believe in a better society. For example, in a communist society, the mindset of an East German would believe: An important heart surgeon walks into a local store and says to himself: "This week I performed four heart surgeries, conducted two important lectures, and saved two lives—I will buy steaks and wine for dinner. That's what I *deserve* because I have *contributed* to society."

Second, by allowing other political parties associated with socialist and communist ideology within the Party Congress and Central Committee was the proof the SED needed the German Democratic Republic was indeed democratic in nature—democratic in the definition associated within the definition of socialism. Even though eight minority political parties were allowed to participate at various government levels, they were never able to change the status quo of the larger SED. Each smaller political party attracted different segments of the East German population, effectively representing the countries interests and needs (Fritz 2009).

Table 2.1 Characteristics of the Communist Political/Economic System

Political System	Totalitarian regime (total control)
Economic System	Command or planned economy
Social Policy country	Party acts in best interest of
Limitations duction	No reward or incentive for pro-

Source: Larry Krieger et al. 1994.

UNDERSTANDING THE EAST GERMAN COMMUNIST MODEL OF GOVERNMENT

The East German political system was largely modeled after the Soviet Union. Under the characteristics of a totalitarian regime, control of all government apparatuses remained firmly in the hands of the political elite (see Figure 2.1).

Figure 2.1 General Structure of the Soviet/East German Government

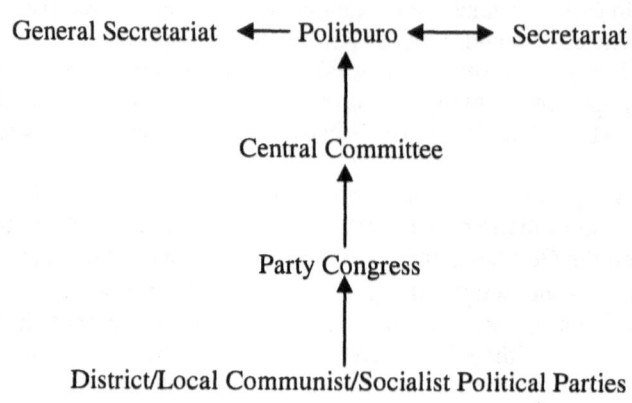

At the lowest level or first level of government were the district and local political parties. While each party catered to the interests of their particular constituents (e.g., workers, farmers, youth, religious organizations), all were required to model and support the basic tenements of communism. With a number of seats allocated to each party, the SED maintained a numerical advantage with 127 seats, followed by the Free German Trade Union with sixty-eight seats, the Christian Democratic Union, National Democratic Party of Germany, the Liberal Democratic Party of Germany, and the Democratic Farmer's Party all maintaining fifty-two seats. The remaining three smaller political parties—the Free German Youth with forty seats, the Democratic Women's League of Germany with thirty-five seats, and the Cultural Association of the GDR with twenty-two seats—maintained a smaller, minority political footprint.

Selected participants from both districts and Local Political Parties were sent as representatives to the Party Congress, which is the second level of government. Usually only meeting once every five years, the Party Congress consisted of five hundred members and was considered to be representative of the people and often established the direction and ideology for extended periods of time. Members of the Party Congress were responsible for the election of representatives to the Central Committee and the appointment of committee members to selected ministries chaired by senior Politburo members.

The Central Committee or the third level of government was the "checks and balances" and the "soundboard" of ideas within the Communist party. Central Committee members meet four times a year to discuss diverse views from throughout the GDR and provide technical reports for senior members of the Communist party and Politburo while working closely with the Secretariat on a regular basis. In addition, the Central Committee regularly carries out decisions and ideological beliefs of the Party Congress when it's not in session. The Central Committee is generally dominated by members of the SED.

Senior members of the Central Committee are often elected to serve in the Politburo. The Politburo is the fourth and highest level of government and is considered the ruling elite within the GDR. Meeting once a week, senior members address party, state, economic, military, and foreign policy issues that affect the country. All members were required to serve on various ministries (boards or councils) dealing with various aspects of the economy, military, foreign policy, health, etc.

The "working arm" within the Politburo is the Secretariat. The Secretariat is staff members in charge with implementing or enacting the policies approved by the Politburo. Working in close relation with the Central Committee, the secretariat staff does the daily operations of the Politburo. Such positions are held by senior members. Lastly, the general secretariat is considered the elected figure of the GDR. Considered a senior member of the Politburo, the General Secretariat is the equivalent to a prime minister or president in western democracies and is widely known as the figure of the country.

THE MENTALITY OF POWER AND CONTROL

With its creation as a nation state in 1949, the GDR relied heavily on the Soviet Union for military security and economic and social support. Since most of the country's natural resources and industries were shipped to the Soviet Union in 1945 and 1946, the Soviet Union was viewed as both the protector and the provider. Thus, in the minds of the Soviet government, the GDR was democratic only in the sense that rule was centralized at the top rather than from the people. A strong, centralized communist government would thus govern for all East German citizens. According to Fulbrook (1997), the GDR was especially reliant upon the Soviet Union in its early years as a nation because (1) East Germany had a substantial amount of Soviet troops (300,000) stationed on GDR soil to both maintain the GDR's political legitimacy and defend against a conflict against the West in central Europe and (2) throughout German history, the German people were obedient to the secular leadership, either good or bad. The sins of the oppressor were thus complemented by the sins of the oppressed.

In an effort to guarantee its very survival, the SED played an active role in the everyday life of East Germans. Beginning with widespread participation at all levels of society (workplace, residential living, recreation, and education), the Communist party stressed a reliance on a grass-roots message to keep alive its message of a better socialist society. As a result, with the military support (protection) from the Soviet Union, the SED justified its legitimacy and very presence by:

1. Adopting the "father" role to protect East German citizens' real interest against foreign and domestic influences.
2. The economic chaos after World War II, the rule of Hitler, and the Weimer Republic all indicated the failure and potential evils of capitalism. Socialism was viewed as a system for the people, to the people.
3. The potential of a revolution from inside threats within the GDR from suspected Fascists resulted in active purges of the "class enemy" until the mid-1950s.
4. The growing power of West Germany and its acceptance of capitalist views in the eyes of the GDR only supported and continued the Nazi past.
5. A pawn of the Soviet Union as East Germany remained the "crown jewel" of the Soviet Union. As the Russian economy grew and fell, so did the East German economy.

LESSON AND ACTIVITIES

The following lessons are designed to reinforce materials found in this chapter in partnership with the school-adopted content textbook. The following lessons should be used as supplemental texts and lessons in an effort to increase cognition over issues associated with the creation of the East German state. With this in mind, multiple styles of lessons and levels of learning are provided, each covering content material related to critical issues faced with post-war Germany. Lesson One, "The East German Dilemma," is a content-centered forced choice lesson that provides students with values-related dilemmas associated with the aftermath of World War II and newly enacted Soviet control of the Russian zone of Germany. Lesson Two, "The _____ Democratic Republic," is an inductive inquiry lesson designed to foster inquiry about the credibility and possibilities of an East German model government model in the students' school. Finally, Lesson Three, "Tough Decisions in the GDR," is a persisting issues lesson with value dilemmas faced by the newly formed East German government in the immediate years following the war.

The East German Dilemma—Classification Lesson

Perched on the ninth floor of the newly established Soviet Military Administration (SMA) in the heart of the Russian-controlled sector of East Germany, General Marshall Zhukov observes the total destruction of four years of ruthless fighting. Berlin, before the war, was considered a progressive, fast-paced city complete with world famous zoos, museums, and parks. However, most if not all of the Russian zone of Eastern Germany lay in ruins. The millions of residents in the Russian-occupied zone lacked the basic necessities to maintain the basic standards of living.

Moreover, the increasing reconstruction and growth of both the western zones of Germany and Berlin by the allied powers of the United States, England, and France has created a negative image for Stalin and leading Communist party members in Moscow. As a result, in the western zones of occupation, an important effort to provide food, water, cooking fuel, and clothing to the battered German people. General Zhukov does not easily forget the destruction and millions of dead at the hands of German troops during the war.

Rebuilding the "Russian zone" of East Germany will not be easy. It is clear to General Zhukov that without some form of aid to the East German people, the possibility of establishing a communist puppet state will be difficult. The strategy will call for an overall reshaping of East Germany socially, politically, and economically while still funneling important resources to Russia in an effort to rebuild its economy.

Receiving pressure from Moscow, General Zhukov is concerned about the "balancing act" of robbing East Germany of its resources while attempting to establish a productive relationship with the German people. Moscow is demanding possible actions taken by Zhukov and the SMA. There are many choices to be made; however, they are not without consequences. Each choice given by General Zhukov will have both a potential positive and negative impact on the demoralized East German people.

Deciding Factors: Which of the following actions do you believe is most important and least important in the overall development of East Germany and East Berlin? The twelve possible actions are as follows:

1. In an effort to reduce hunger, 20% of the food produced in the Soviet Union will be sent to the people of East Germany.
2. In an effort to "repay" for the German sins of war, all forms of heavy industry will be disassembled and shipped back to the Soviet Union.
3. In an effort to have better accountability of food production and light industry, the SMA, along with members of the German Communist party, will "take over" all means of food and industrial production.
4. In an effort to "repay" for the German sins of war, all forms of agriculture will be collective (government-controlled) with 10% shipped back to the Soviet Union.

5. Focus all of East Germany's remaining natural resources into the Russian zone in Berlin to match various reconstruction plans made by the Americans, British, and French.
6. Increase oil and coal shipments to East Germany in return for cooperation in the political, social, and economic transformation to a communist form of government.
7. Begin the overall development of East Germany with the educational system. Remove all discussion of religion, personal desires, and replace content with cooperation, community, and government.
8. Let the East Germans run the show. Allow East German communists to find and relocate anticommunists and then develop their own country based on East German communist views. Russia would provide financial and political support to maintain a large communist presence. All political opposition would be crushed.
9. Encourage German citizens to become members of the Communist party. Non-communist members will be blocked from higher education and premier jobs.
10. Provide everyone able-working East German citizen with a government-supported/-controlled job.
11. Provide all members of the Communist party an opportunity to attend a higher education institution or career training.
12. Provide all German citizens with proper housing and reliable ground transportation (trains).

Instead of performing all of the actions above, General Zhukov must decide what is realistic and unrealistic. Thus he must decide on the following:

Three most likely to work:
1.
2.
3.

Three least likely to work:
1.
2.
3.

Alternative fit (neither):
1.
2.

Inquiry Lesson Example: The (_____) Democratic Republic— Inquiry Lesson

For the Teacher:
In a world of various competing models of government, most students find the actual inner-workings to be difficult, at best, to understand. This lesson is designed to provide students with an insight on how, *in theory*, communist model might be implemented at a personal level. Using pre-existing organizations, roles, and policies already established in your school, this lesson asks the students to take such established roles and create, *in theory*, a small communist model. The desired goal for this lesson is not to necessarily endorse or create an actual working communist model of government, but rather *personalize* such a model on a level that students might better understand.

Step 1: A question is raised and stated clearly.
Ask the class what type of government their school has. Does the school have a student council or government? Are all groups, organizations, and students fairly represented? Would a better or different model of student government work?

Step 2: A tentative answer is developed.
Encourage a class discussion on the strengths and weaknesses of your school's current structure. Oddly enough, what most schools consider a "student council," in fact, is not a council but rather a loose interpretation of government. Ask students (either in small groups or as a whole class) if they believe the East German model of government *could* or *would* work at their school level? What would they believe the potential strengths or weaknesses would be? Brainstorm school organizations that could be represented at the (a) district level, (b) Party Congress, (c) Central Committee, and (d) Politburo.

Step 3: Evidence bearing on the tentative answer is gathered.
Either in small groups or individually, provide students with the handout titled, "The Basic Structure of the East German Government" and any additional notes given in class or readings. Ask students to brainstorm of all the social clubs, organizations, and student representation at their school. After doing so, ask the students to insert such organizations based on the models provided in the handout titled, "High School Democratic Republic."

Step 4: A conclusion is drawn from the evidence.
Have students or groups present their individual models to the class. Ask students to discuss their diagrams and possible strengths and weaknesses.

Step 5: Conclusion is applied to the original question.
On the board, conduct a class discussion and illustrate the overall strengths and weaknesses of using the East German model at their school or why their current form of student government is more suitable.

The Basic Structure of the East German Government

At the lowest level or first level of government were the district and local political parties. While each party catered to the interests of their particular constituents (e.g., workers, farmers, youth, religious organizations), all were required to model and support the basic tenements of communism. With a number of seats allocated to each party, the SED maintained a numeric advantage with 127 seats, followed by the Free German Trade Union with sixty-eight seats, the Christian Democratic Union, the National Democratic Party of Germany, the Liberal Democratic Party of German, and the Democratic Farmer's Party, all maintaining fifty-two seats. The remaining three smaller political parties—Free German Youth with forty seats, Democratic Women's League of Germany with thirty-five seats, and the Cultural Association of the GDR with twenty-two seats—maintained a smaller, minority political footprint.

Selected participants from both districts and local political parties were sent as representatives to the Party Congress which is the second level of government. Usually only meeting once every five years, the Party Congress consisted of 500 members and was considered to be representative of the people and often established the direction and ideology for extended periods of time. Members of the Party Congress were responsible for the election of representatives to the Central Committee and the appointment of committee members to selected ministries chaired by senior Politburo members.

The Central Committee or the third level of government was the "checks and balances" and the "soundboard" of ideas within the Communist party. Central Committee members meet four times a year to discuss diverse views from throughout the GDR and provide technical reports for senior members of the Communist party and Politburo, while working closely with the Secretariat on a regular basis. In addition, the Central Committee regularly carries out decisions and ideological beliefs of the Party Congress when it's not in session. The Central Committee is generally dominated by members of the SED.

Senior members of the Central Committee are often elected to serve in the Politburo. The Politburo is the fourth and highest level of government and is considered the ruling elite within the GDR. Meeting once a week, senior members address party, state, economic, military, and foreign policy issues that affect the country. All members are required to serve on various ministries (boards or councils) dealing with various aspects of the economy, military, foreign policy, health, etc.

The "working arm" within the Politburo is the Secretariat. The Secretariat consists of staff members in charge with implementing or enacting the policies approved by the Politburo. Working in close relation with the Central Committee, the secretariat staff does the daily operations of the Politburo. Such positions are held by senior members. Lastly, the general secretariat is considered the elected figure of the GDR. Considered a senior member of the Politburo, the General Secretariat is the equivalent to a prime minister or president in western democracies and is widely known as the figure of the country.

High School Democratic Republic

The following model is intended to represent how the East German model of government *might* work in a typical high school setting. Like the official model, school representation is divided among clubs, organizations, and committees. In the end, the model may provide representation for the student body.

At the lowest or first level of the school model consists of clubs and organizations. Such groups (all recognized by the administration within your school) are allowed to provide between five and eight students supporting each organization's interest during the first week of school. The number of representatives varies according to your schools number of clubs and organizations. Such representatives will then meet in the Party Congress.

The Party Congress of _____ High School or second level of the school model is made up of representatives from your school's clubs and organizations. The total number of representatives will vary according to your school's number of groups. Regardless, the Party Congress meets once at the beginning of each semester. It is the Party's job to establish the *general* direction of the school for all grades. Selected members in the Party Congress are invited to sit on school committees. The Party Congress at the beginning of the year will elect students to serve on Central Committee.

The Central Committee of _____ High School or the third level of the model government is made up of twenty representatives elected directly from the Party Congress. Elected students who serve in the Central Committee generally are junior or seniors. Committee members meet four times a semester to review the work of the Politburo and Secretariat and are considered the "checks and balances" for the Politburo. In addition, Central Committee members carry out the vision of the Party Congress when they are not in session. Finally, the Central Committee provides information on school matters such as recommendations, concerns, etc. Members in the Central Committee elect the Politburo.

The Politburo of _____ High School or the fourth level of the school model consists of a total of seven students directly elected from the Central Committee. Five students are members of the working Politburo. These five juniors and seniors are those who have "worked through" the system. All five members along with the General Secretariat and Secretariat must have a consensus vote. Members meet once every two weeks to address school issues such as entertainment issues, fund-raising, elections, school affairs, etc. Each of the five members serves and chairs various school committees along with selected students in the Party Congress. All recommendations made by the Politburo are sent to the Central Committee for review. Two students are elected within the Politburo to become the Secretariat. These two students send all policies via e-mail to the Central Committee, meet with the administration, and provide notes and reports when needed. Finally, the General Secretariat is elected within the Politburo to be the school president. This individual meets with the school's administration and is the overall voice of the student body and is the "face" of the school.

Tough Decisions in the GDR—Persisting Issues Lesson

Directions: As a high-ranking member of the newly formed Socialist Unity Party (SED) in East Germany, your political party has several immediate problems facing your nation. Below is a list of problems. Rank the potential response with "1" being the best choice, "2" being the second best choice, etc.

Problem: There is a food shortage throughout East Germany (GDR). The Soviet Union has limited food shipments to your country and demands your government resolves the problem.
Alternatives available:
   A. Ration food on a weekly basis. Members and East Germans who join your party receive first selections on food.
   B. Limit supplies of food in the rural areas of the GDR and provide East Berlin (the symbol of your new country) with the most food to "illustrate" to the West your country's wealth.
   C. Encourage farmers to surrender their land and join together to produce food products more efficiently.
   D. Take over the transportation and distribution process in the GDR to make it more efficient and available to the people.

Problem: Your political party wants to win the "hearts and minds" of the East German people in an effort to keep communism in place.
Alternatives available:
   A. Illustrate to the East Germans how Hitler's view of capitalism failed.
   B. Indicate that due to your country's close alliance with the Soviet Union, as their economy grows, so too does East Germany's.
   C. Begin introducing the concept of communism in the country's schools and eliminate all other teachings of government.
   D. Tell the East German people that your government has their best interests at heart; give each family special privilege if they join the SED.

Problem: East German citizens are skeptical of your political party's political and economic systems of total control and a planned (government-controlled) economy.
Alternatives available:
   A. Provide each family with a guaranteed job with benefits.
   B. Provide each family with free health care.
   C. Provide members of the Communist party with special privileges such as acceptance to college, higher paying jobs, and larger apartments.
   D. Begin a new education campaign in the nation's schools that teaches only about the benefits of communism. All students are encouraged to join communist-related youth organizations and attend communist-related activities to ensure acceptance into college or vocational training.

THREE

THE ENEMY FROM WITHIN: THE FORMATION OF THE STASI

A Brief History of the Ministry for State Security (Stasi)

The Ministry for State Security (MfS) or Stasi was established in 1950 as the small, personal protection force of both the Socialist Unity Party (SED) and its leadership. Originally modeled after the occupying Soviet Secret Police (NKVD), the MfS protected sensitive government buildings and party officials with the sole purpose of being the "shield and sword" of the Communist party. During the first three years of its existence, the MfS maintained a small secret police organization with a limited budget. However, the Stasi's role and importance grew dramatically after the failed 1953 uprising by workers and farmers angered by the lack of goods and services offered by the SED. With aid from the Russian military, the uprising was crushed, leaving the SED fearful of future uprisings and its political future. This potentially fatal uprising against a fledgling communist government persuaded Politburo members to increase the overall powers and authority of the MfS to ensure total control of enemies both foreign and local. Now, maintaining control of power, safety, and structure was divided among three government agencies: the National Volksarmee, the Volkspolizie, and the Stasi.

The National Volksarmee (military) was a Soviet-backed standing military founded under the principle to protect East German workers and farmers against all enemies abroad. In addition, the National Volksarmee would host 300,000 Russian soldiers on East German soil as an active deterrent against possible aggression from western (NATO) forces. The regular East German police (Volkspolizie) included criminal and patrolling police that handled daily, convential crimes and homicides. The Stasi's role was to dramatically increase in both funding and responsibility. After 1953, the Stasi increased its mission from guarding government buildings and political leaders to a more active role in monitoring internal and external activities regarded as potential threats to the GDR.

Stasi agents conducted internal espionage operations against all dissenting views in East Germany. Technical eavesdropping along with secretly opening citizens' mail were the two most common methods of gathering information against enemies of the State. To maintain the growing fear of external sabotage from West Germany and its allies, the Stasi were instructed to conduct espionage missions and counter-espionage missions to gather information, assassinate political leaders, and recruit spies to gather sensitive secret information. In an effort to maintain strict control of traffic and individuals entering and leaving East Germany, the Stasi maintained a secret presence at all border crossings, effectively ensuring strict regulation on passport control.

However, such demand and growth expected by the SED required enormous amounts of resources. Increased budgets, creation of regional Stasi districts and offices, and increased manpower effectively made the MfS the most feared organization in East Germany and one of the most effective spy agencies in the world. Such growth did not happen overnight. Over a forty-year period, it grew from a small protection force into a massive organization (bureaucracy) of over 90,000 full-time employees devoted to defending socialism.

The Development of the Stasi Headquarters and State Bureaucracy

In 1989 when the Berlin Wall fell and ruling SED was all but lost, the Stasi had employed over 97,000 full-time employees—more than a sufficient number of agents to oversee a nation of 17,000,000 residents. In addition to the full-time members, the MfS also employed 173,000 part-time unofficial informers (IMs) among the population. During the era of Hitler, it was estimated that there was one Gestapo agent for every 2,000 citizens and in the Soviet Union, there one KGB (secret police) agent for every 5,380 citizens. In East Germany, a Stasi agent was assigned for every 63 East Germans, and if "part-time" informants are considered, the number was closer to one for every 6.5 citizens. The end result was nearly 15,000 Stasi bureaucrats working each day in administration activities to conduct overseas espionage and domestic surveillance in 15 regional districts and 200 local offices to ensure the safety of the Communist party (Funder 2003).

To achieve such an astonishing number of agents, the MfS selected only the best candidates. In theory, individuals couldn't actually apply. Rather, the Ministry recruited and carefully selected candidates that had passed all of the preliminary exams, and were members of the SED. It was this loyalty to the SED and East Germany that created the need to investigate others. According to SED leadership, all dissenting views from East Germans came from outside imperialist forces. Such undesirable political views required intense operations against the East German people by the MfS effectively provided the Stasi a "green light" to monitor all citizens and institutions (e.g., the economy, State apparatus, Church, sports, culture) and counter terrorism in efforts to protect the Communist party. The department of Church was the only area in East German society where oppositional thought (free thinkers) could find structure and share similar anticommunist beliefs. As a result, theological colleges attracted intelligent, creative, and independent thinkers. Often, Stasi agents and IMs would infiltrate theological institutions to recruit students. In all, 65% of Church pastors were informers for the Stasi while the remaining 35% were under surveillance (Funder 2003).

Internal and External Espionage Operations

The monitoring of all citizens in East Germany took massive resources. According to Rückel (2008), at the peak of Stasi domestic surveillance, some 280,000 politically related verdicts were delivered, 20,000 active phone lines were tapped, and 90,000 letters were opened daily. Such technical eavesdropping (listening devices in individual's homes) provided the most rewarding and valuable information and surveillance for Stasi agents. Other forms of intelligence-gathering were collecting through informers, shadow surveillance (following suspects), blackmail, and open investigations. Results of gathered information were documented in a national database where 39,000 citizens had index cards containing suspected activities deemed antisocialist.

Individuals taken into Stasi custody were often done so in the early morning hours, with most being told they are being detained for "clarification of facts" in a cell with no windows. The art of "disintegration elective" was commonly used on selected subjects before their arrest. The practice of disintegrating someone by destroying the subjects' self-esteem and through misfortunes (e.g., losing their job, creating a divorce through false information) without the individual knowing who was creating these problems simply "softened" subjects before lengthy interrogations in their own prison system separate from the Volkspolizie.

Once processed into the Stasi prison, a subject was given one of three political opponent labels: (1) Hostile Person, (2) Hostile Negative Person, or (3) Hardened Hostile Negative Person (who was lost to East German society and often imprisoned for life). The goal of the Stasi was for citizens to never be placed in either of these categories but rather to "nip" most problems through disintegration. For prisoners who fell under one of the three political opponent categories, they were never informed of their charges. While confessions were the easiest way of conviction, prisoners awaiting trial were encouraged to collect information on fellow inmates in the hope of lighter sentences.

Courts were influenced by Stasi officials. Few trials lasted more than one day. After sentencing, convicted political prisoners were sent to designate Stasi prisons where each prisoner was monitored every five minutes while in their cells. Here, the Stasi continued their surveillance of political prisoners through a "total surveillance" network designed to gain further information (see Table 3.1). The concept of "total surveillance" consisted of Stasi members spying on the prison staff. Prison staff members would spy on the inmates, and in return, the inmates were recruited to spy on other inmates and staff members, creating a circle of surveillance.

Figure 3.1 Stasi Total Surveillance

East Germans themselves were also an intricate part of internal espionage. The MfS acknowledges that while its organization maintained a significant number of full-time agents, total surveillance would be difficult. As a result, the Stasi relied on IMs to gather intelligence on family members, friends, and colleagues. Spezialdisziplin was the science of recruiting informers. According to Fritz (2009), the majority of IMs received a small payment for their services (gathering information on others) or unofficial recognition from the government through a medal, letter, etc. Most East Germans didn't turn down the Stasi when asked to inform on others. When needed, the Stasi would use blackmail or damaging information to "encourage" members of society to work for the Stasi when asked. However, the majority of citizens did not require forceful encouragement to gather information on their fellow East Germans. In short, most East Germans either truly believed in socialism or they were opportunistic and believed it was easier to further one's career knowing the Stasi were supporting you.

The wide range of the MfS's foreign activity was directed toward West Germany in the form of political, military, and industrial espionage (Gieseke 2006). Since East Germany was politically and socially incapable of expanding communism as a whole to West Germany, there were active attempts to influence national elections and the small minority Communist party through "disinformation and psychological warfare against the west." The HVA division of the Stasi was responsible for western espionage. Unlike agents operating in East Germany, HVA agents wore suits instead of uniforms and were multilingual, highly educated people who blended well into their western surroundings. According to Funder (2003), much of the Stasi's energy and efforts were directed at West Germany, in which both sensitive and secret information was collected from working agents in the west and leaked to cause harm against West German politicians. The Stasi manufactured documents and spliced together audio recordings of conversations that never existed in efforts to harm politicians in the public sphere; they also spread rumors that politicians worked for them. In addition, the HVA fed false misleading information to western news outlets about the Nazi past of West German political leaders (which was extremely effective); it funded communist-related publications and made various attempts to alter election outcomes.

LESSON AND ACTIVITIES

The following lessons are designed to reinforce materials found in this chapter in partnership with the school-adopted content textbook. The following lessons should be used as supplemental text and lessons in an effort to increase cognition over issues associated with the MfS. With this in mind, multiple styles of lessons and levels of learning are provided, each covering content material related to critical issues faced by Stasi agents. Lesson One, "How I Became an Unofficial Informer," is a persisting issues lesson that provides students with a value dilemma associated with working for the MfS. Lesson Two, "The West German Spies Dilemma," is a case study lesson designed to highlight various activities and espionage information gathered by Stasi agents. Lesson Three, "Operation Torch Light: East Germany's Policy for the Protestant Church," is a persisting issues lesson that forces students to make values decisions over Stasi operations within the Church. Lesson Four, "Antigovernment Activities: What Would You Do?" is a content-centered, forced-choice lesson that provide students with a variety of choices in efforts to monitor and discourage antigovernment activities. Lastly, Lesson Five, "Demoralization Measures," is a persisting issues lesson designed to expose students to Stasi measures to take advantage of hostile-negative citizens.

How I Became an Unofficial Informer (IM)—Persisting Issues Lesson

Directions: Below is the case of a high school student living in East Germany who was approached and recruited to become an "unofficial informer." Read this short story. After doing so, decide, in your opinion, if this student did the appropriate action.

One day in April 1986, my school principal had me sent to the office. At first, I panicked, wondering what I had done. Was it skipping class, not doing my homework, or even smoking? In fact, I wasn't in trouble at all. My school principal wanted to introduce me to Mr. B. Once my principal made the formal introduction, he left. At first I thought Mr. B was a mechanic who had slipped into a suit; he had a small, chubby face and hands indicating that he worked outside and used them often. He appeared young, but I could tell he had been out of school for some time. He said he wanted to talk to me about several of the students in our school. At first I thought he might be in some leadership role with the Free German Youth Organization, but he didn't fit the image. He said he knew I was popular among different students and knew everybody well. He admitted that he knew little about the students because nobody would talk to him since he was an adult. In an effort to locate students who were "different," he was hoping to have private conversations with individual students like myself on a regular basis. It was a strange situation. He asked about certain students—what they did after school and more importantly, what they talked about when they attended church. What could I tell Mr. B that he didn't already know? How should I help him? Do I lie about students to him? At the end of our conversation, he told me he worked for the Ministry for State Security (Stasi) and that regardless of my decision, I couldn't tell anyone of our conversation, not even my parents. After Mr. B left, I became upset. Everyone knew who and what the Stasi did. The Stasi was a part of everyday life, much like family, school, church, etc.

Part of me was scared to talk to the Stasi, and the other part of me was curious and in a weird way, honored that they had come to me for information. Before I decided to "inform on others," I was required to write a declaration of commitment as an unofficial informer before I could receive any money for information. My declaration of commitment was the following:

I, _____, resident in Mitte, German Democratic Republic, voluntarily pledge to cooperate with Mfs (Stasi). I am prepared to report to the MfS in written and oral form about all things aimed against the security of the State. I will maintain absolute secrecy regarding this pledge towards all individuals. I have been instructed that violation of this pledge can cause harm to East Germany and I can be punished (for doing so). To preserve secrecy, I select the name Walter Uhlm.

Mr. B and I met regularly. I provided him information about students who often spoke negatively about the government. Mr. B appreciated the information and often told me how I was helping to protect the country from traitors and Western influences. Regardless of the information I provided, Mr. B regularly asked about what my friends did and when they attended church. He wanted to know if any of the students were being influenced by church members or the clergy and about the readings that were given to us. I was beginning to have questions about why Mr. B was so interested in youth activities at church. The only thing I knew was that I particularly liked the pastor at our local church. I didn't want to tell Mr. B anything about the people, the pastor, or his wife that would get them in trouble.

After reading the story, what would you do?
1. Would you agree with the student's decision to become an IM and provide potentially valuable information about his friends and others? Why?
2. Suppose the school's principal asked for this information rather than Mr. B. Would this make a difference?
3. When is it okay to provide information about others? Why?
4. What do you believe are the reasons the student provided information?
5. Is it ever okay for the government to gather information on others? Why?

The West German Spies Dilemma—Case Study Lesson

For the Teacher: Teaching about the Cold War, specifically about tensions between the Eastern Bloc and Western Europe, may be difficult. This case study affords you the ability to use the case study strategy in an effort to illustrate the knowledge, resourcefulness, and creativity used by the East German Secret Police (Stasi) to maintain their "socialist utopian state." This lesson is designed to both broaden students' cooperative skills and increase their level of critical inquiry. In efforts to guide one through this lesson, steps are provided below.

Step 1: Introduction.
To "set the stage" for this lesson, it is recommended that students are put into groups of three or four. Inform the students that the year is 1965 and they are spies working undercover in East Berlin. They have been working for the West German government for several years, providing excellent information. However, your handler (the West German government) would like to have additional information on ALL aspects of the Stasi and their abilities to gather secret information. You have received a "once-in-a-lifetime opportunity." After following a Stasi agent for weeks, your team has stumbled onto some valuable information. You will only have *fifteen minutes* to investigate each of the documents. Your goal is for the Stasi agent not to discover his documents have been compromised. Now, your team has to decide what is important. There are NO set criteria on what is considered valuable, so you must work as a team.

Step 2: Learning experience distributed.
Provide each group with their instruction sheet document and ten documents. Each document deals with unique situations and operations conducted by Stasi agents both in East and West Germany. Information is diverse, much like most Stasi operations. Indicate to the class that they have a total of *fifteen minutes* to analyze, evaluate, and select the most valuable documents. The key issues are "What is important?" and "What is not?"

Step 3: Comprehension development.
Allow students to evaluate each document. Provide students with the information sheet. Students are to only select (photograph) the *three most important documents*. Students are also instructed to rank the importance of the remaining seven documents. It is important to understand that there are no set criteria for the value of each document. Students are to determine the importance and *perceived* value by West German authorizes. Students are to defend their selections.

Step 4: Reinforcement/Extension.
Ask each group to identify and explain their top three documents. After each group has completed their selections, inform students (through discussion or notes) how and why East Germany was so resourceful in its spying operations throughout the world and on its own people.

The West German Spies Dilemma

The date is 15 May 1965. For the past two years, you and your friends have secretly worked for the West German Military by spying on the East Berlin's Ministerium fur Staatssicherheit (Stasi) headquarters and high ranking officials in the SED.

Your team has collected excellent information in the past, and recently, your information has been "noticed" at higher levels of the West German government. Your team has recently been tasked to follow several "medium-level" Stasi agents whom you believe have a mix of interesting information regarding the West along with situations dealing with civil rights and espionage issues within East Germany. As your team follows one of your "identified" agents, you find the rare opportunity to "liberate" a briefcase when the Stasi agent is preoccupied. With briefcase in hand, your team makes a quick break to one of your predetermined safe houses.

Once the situation seems safe, you realize the importance of examining and selecting what you believe is the most important information to send back to West Berlin. You know it will not be long before the Stasi agent will reluctantly report the missing documents. Now, time is NOT on your side. Your employer (West Germany) needs good information on ALL aspects of East Germany. Your information can provide valuable information about this closed society. It is up to your team to decide what is important and what is not.

When you open the folder, you find ten documents dealing with a range of issues. Instead of sending all of the documents to your West German handler, you are only allowed to *take photographs* of what your team believes are the *three most important documents*. Remember, information is important, and time is NOT on your side. It's only a matter of time before the Volkspolizie (Police) will begin their search of each building. Now you must rank the importance of each document. You will be asked to justify your decision!

The three most important documents (high priority) to be sent to West Berlin with your film are:
   1.
   2.
   3.

The three documents of importance (medium priority) that you would send if you had more film are:
   1.
   2.
   3.

The three documents of low importance (low priority) that you would send if you had lots of extra film are:
1.
2.
3.

How did your team decide on the importance of each document?

What did your team decide what is important: Military information or information on East German citizens?

In your opinion, which had greater value: information about civilians or government activity?

Case #1

Subject: Internal espionage activities
Name: Heinrich Lummner (Case #52209)
Date of arrest: 22 May 1963
Charge: Activities (espionage) against the GDR and the socialist people of East Germany.
Informant: Mark Jakobs (Sergeant 7th border guards)

Allegations to crime(s):
Heinrich Lummner was arrested on 22 May 1963 for suspicion of espionage for the Central Intelligence Agency (CIA) and West German Intelligence. Heinrich, age twenty years, was assigned to the northern border district/sector in East Berlin. Heinrich completed initial infantry training and border guard assignment training on 5 October 1962. Both parents are active members in the Sozialistische Einheitspartei (East German Socialist Unity Party) and were considered supporters until the date of arrest. On 7 January 1963, a Stasi informant indicated Lummner making anti-Party comments. Lummner was reported saying "the socialist party oppresses the peace loving people of East German." Informant (code name: Farmer) also indicated Lummner referred to the Berlin Wall as Schandmauer (Wall of Shame). Additional reports from Farmer indicated Lummner's increasing interest in Stasi surveillance of strategic areas along northern wall fortifications. It is believed by informants within Lummner's border guard unit that Heinrich is sending vital Wall defenses to members in West Berlin. Two Stasi agents were "assigned" to unit. Activity ceased. On 15 April 1963, Stasi agent (code name: Gustuff) intercepted a hand-written note written by Lummner on 10 April 1963 to West German radio station XXXXX. Gustuff indicates letter describes the "oppressive state" of the East German Socialist Party and system." Furthermore, Lummner describes economic conditions found in the motherland. Note was allegedly thrown over Berlin Wall in glass bottle.

Gustuff indicated additional notes found from three GDR soldiers in middle and southern sectors of the Wall.

Actions taken/directed:
Evidence was "sufficient" for conviction. Three men arrested and imprisoned from unit:
- Joseph Thierfeld: One year of hard labor for failure to report crimes against the State. Hans Schmidt: One year of hard labor for failure to report crimes against the State.
- Ekkehard Schultz: One year of hard labor for failure to report crimes against the State.
- Heinrich Lummner: Twenty years of hard labor for espionage activities.
- Mark Jacobs: Promotion to 1st Sergeant and transfer to southern sector.

Method(s) of confession:
Deprivation of food and water for twenty-four hours. Exposure to the elements, isolation (twenty-one days), and revocation of parent's Socialist party status.

Conclusion:
Tighter control of border guard selection must be present. Failure to maintain proper control of border sectors increases probability of illegal border crossings in Northern sectors of the Wall fortifications. Increased Stasi presence is requested. Northern sectors (Bornholmer District) of wall fortifications are secure with increase risk of future disruptions.

Case #2

Subject:	Crimes against the People (illegal distribution of propaganda)
Name:	Walter Erdmann (Case #1007)
Date of arrest:	12 November 1962
Charge:	False claims/capitalist propaganda against the GDR and the socialist people of East Germany.
Informant:	Hans Christophersten (2nd-year medical student)

Allegations to crime(s):
Walter Erdmann, age twenty-one years and second-year medical student at the University Greifswald, was charged with anti-Party activity. During the night of 7 November, Erdmann along with another student (Hans Klauk) placed antisocialist fliers across the school's campus. Previous reports (background checks dated 3 May 1958, 24 October 1960, and 5 May 1962) indicate loyalty to party, resulting in study of medicine. Informant Hans Christophersten indicated Erdmann's numerous discussions of illegal travels to West Berlin while on "university travels" and possible illegal entrance into West Berlin through a false compartment in Trablant or Fiat. Both students were detained (forcefully) and inter-

rogated. Confession to crimes was recorded for Mikel Schmidt (accomplice to Erdmann) on 13 November. Erdmann did not confess and was isolated (in nude) for twenty-four hours. Transported to political prisoners ward on 15 November for "re-education activities." Political prisoner is currently receiving physical rehabilitation.

Actions taken/directed:
Evidence was "sufficient" for conviction.
- Hans Klauk given five years of hard labor.
- Ingrid Klauk, mother, given six months of hard labor for failure to report crime(s) against the GDR.
- Walter Erdmann given ten years hard labor and political re-education.
- Hans Christophersten to receive top choice (locations) for medical assignment.

Method(s) of confession:
Deprivation of food and water for twenty-four hours. Exposure to the elements, physical conditioning (encouragement), and investigations of family members.

Conclusion:
Closer examination of medical students required. Possibility of medical travels to West Berlin must be investigated further. Guards along all sectors encouraged to search vehicles entering and leaving East Berlin.

Case #3

Subject: Terrorist Activities
Name: Josef Kneifel (Case #82234)
Date of arrest: 10 April, 1963
Charge: False Claims against the GDR and Socialist Cause
Informant: Classified

Allegations to crime(s):
On 5 April 1963, Josef Kneifel, a factory worker at The Parties Steel Factory outside of East Berlin is skilled as both a welder and lathe operator. Kneifel was a top performer at the factory. Skills considered valuable. Warned several times about his "anti-Party" language by shift supervisor. On 7 April 1963, Kneifel told local priest at location XXXX that "East Germans have prostituted themselves to Moscow" and "the socialist cause and state was ruthless and paranoid in controlling the behavior of the masses."Arrested on 10 April, 1963 by Stasi Agent XXXX and Agent XXXX.

Actions taken/directed:
Evidence was "sufficient" for conviction.
- Joseph Kneifel given ten months of hard labor.
- Irmgard Kneifel given three months of hard labor for failure to report a crime.

Method(s) of confession:
Deprivation of food and water for 24 hours. Exposure to the elements, physical conditioning (encouragement), and investigations of family members.

Conclusion:
Skilled labor is an essential asset to the GDR. Continued monitoring of such labor is crucial. Skilled labor can devise homemade weapons, bombs, and devices that may lead to the increased probability of escape. Successful infiltration into local churches has increased information and possible antigovernment activity. It is recommended local universities continue to be placed under surveillance to include student organizations and athletic groups. It is believed that students are considered the primary threat for future escape attempts.

Case #4

Date: 1 June 1964
Subject: West Berlin Interceptions

Acting on Order No. 2872 from Comrade Mielke, all high-profile escapees from GDR soil are to captured and returned to the GDR or eliminated due to their high security risks of false propaganda against the State. West German youth organizations are of particular interest. The following names have been reported as collaborators against the GDR. Immediate action is requested.

- **Ruth von Stahl**, age twenty-nine years, student at Free Berlin University. Subject has provided "technical assistants" to various Western newspapers regarding Wall fortifications, and detailed surveillance of border guard shift changes.
- **Mikel Dahl**, age twenty-four years, DJ at Freedom Radio located in West Berlin. Subject has played music deemed "subversive" to the Socialist cause. Subject has, on numerous occasions, directed East Berlin citizens to escape and rise up against the GDR.
- **Anna Ulm**, age twenty years, waitress who negotiated border obstacles in 1961. Subject is currently active in raising funds to help East German citizens pay for their freedom.

Case #5

Date: 7 April 1964
Subject: West Berlin Police (captain) (Case #72181)
On 3 March 1963, Stasi agent XXXXXX was successful in the recruitment of a West Berlin detective (Code Name: Fishbed). Fishbed continues to provide the Berlin district with valuable and credible information on the following: personnel structure (leadership/command structure) and retiring and newly hired personnel, personnel structure and strength, readiness orders (number of officers patrolling each shift), intelligence of East German activity, current wanted lists, names of all GDR citizens who currently reside in West Berlin, and access to the West Berlin Central Police Headquarter (wire-tapped phones).

Case #6

Date: 9 June 1964
Subject: West Berlin Police (Communication Sergeant) (Case # 14409)
After the successful recruitment of West Berlin police officer (Code Name: Fishbed), Stasi agent XXXXXX made successful contact with a communication specialist working within the West Berlin central police headquarters. Communications specialist (Code Name: Saturn) has provided the Berlin district with telecommunication codes used to transmit sensitive information dealing with emergency management, emergency response codes and data. The Berlin district has verified all information and has successfully compromised codes on a limited basis.

Case #7

Suspicion: Terrorist activities
Name: Hans Cole (Case #10092)
Date of initial observation: 10 April 1963
Charge: False claims against the GDR and socialist cause
Informant: Classified

Allegations to crime(s):
On 5 April 1963, Cole, a factory worker outside of East Berlin was identified after Cole's shift supervisor contact the Volkspolizie (police) after Hans repeatedly told peers about his willingness to "make a statement" against oppression. Agent XXXX interviewed the shift supervisor and began the initial observation of Cole on 10 April 1963. While at work, Agents XXXX and XXXX successfully entered Cole's home. Black powder and what appear machined tubes with caps were found. Items were photographed and left.

On 14 April 1963, Hans told local priest at location XXXX that "The East Germans government would collapse at the hands of the people" and "the socialist cause and state was ruthless and paranoid in controlling the behavior of the masses."Initial audio recordings within XXXX church suggest Cole is willing to enact harm to either Volkspolizie or Stasi offices.

Case #8

Suspicion: Antigovernment propaganda
Name: Miriam Mundt (Case #00988)
Date of initial
 observation: 6 February 1963
Charge: Enemy of the State
Informant: Christopher Hans

Allegations to crime(s):
Miriam Mundt, age eighteen years, was reported to Stasi officials for allegedly printing antigovernment propaganda against the GDR. On 28 January 1963, Mundt, along with a friend, made and distributed pamphlets to speak up and against local party (government) reforms. Subject allegedly pasted pamphlets at the main train station in Leipzig. Mundt, on 29, placed two pamphlets on Peter Hans, a former schoolmate. Christopher Hans, Peter's father and active member in the Solialistische Einheitspartei (East German Socialist Unity Party), turned the evidence in to Stasi station #325 in Leipzig. On 6 February, agents entered Mundt's residence and found rubber stamp letters that were similar in both font size and letters used on pamphlets.

Case #9

Date: 23 September 1963
Subject: Karl Schmillberg (Case #22345)
Operation: Bavarian homecoming
Karl Schmillberg is employed by the United States Army 427th Military Intelligence Battalion, West Berlin. As a civilian with special security clearances, Schmillberg has access to sensitive information. On 19 September 1963, Schmillberg stole classified documents using a military mailbag. His escape was successful, using false documents prepared by Agent XXXX to enter East Berlin. The significance of Schmillberg's information is as follows:
- Names of 42 American/West German agents working in East Germany.
- Codes to NATO forces scrambled communications (limited).
- American/West German agents monitoring rail yard/railroad operations pertaining to Russian tank transportation.
- Detailed railroad diagrams and communications from the Polish border.

- Monitoring of goods (ammunition, food supplies) used by East German forces.

Case #10

Date: 3 August 1963
Subject: XXXXX (Case #01125)
Operation: Street sweeper

Stasi agent XXXXX successfully penetrated the Bundensnachrichtendienst (BND) (West German Intelligence Service) on 2 February 1963. Agent has gained access to files concerning spying activities conducted in Eastern Europe. Agent reports on various occasions of CIA activity in the GDR seaport of Warnemunde and various railroad activities in Rostock. Agent indicates several Western intelligence officers are embedded and compromised East German/Russian intelligence services at the following military units assigned to defend GDR soil:

- 11th Guards Tank Division located in Dresden
- 34th Engineer Regiment located in East Berlin
- 10th Armor Division located in Potsdam
- 94th Motorized Rifle Division located in Schwerin

Furthermore, Agent indicates Western intelligence has detailed records of troop's strengths, military leave (rotation of soldiers), and current levels of munitions on reserve status.

Operation Torch Light: East Germany's Policy of the Protestant Church—Persisting Issues Lesson

Directions: Read the following paragraph. As a high ranking member of the East German MfS, it's your responsibility to evaluate the following report.

TOP SECRET
Date: 27 October 1988
Subject: Church activities
Operation: Torch light

Churches and religious communities in East Germany (GDR) were considered a thorn in the flesh of our country's Socialist Unity Party's control against Western influences and increased human rights complaints. With the initial conception of our country in 1949, churches have maintained a certain degree of independence. Many churches throughout the GDR have influenced their local towns in terms of actively criticizing government policy and maintaining a safe harbor for environmental, peace, and human rights groups. In addition, the Church is considered an active threat to the GDR because the Church (1) offers strength in retreat (daily living) for East Germans, (2) believes in an afterlife, (3) is able to connect with the masses through outside activities not connected to Church operations, and (4) provides a competing set of values other than communism. Therefore, government policy towards these groups is aimed to stop or at least decrease their influences by means of open or silent repression in the name of national security. Official MfS recommendations include the following actions:

1. Infiltrate Church seminaries (schools) to recruit IMs to provide future information on both fellow clergy and members.
2. Begin a campaign to squeeze out any form of religious education in schools and increase the pressure to conform to government policy through school-based campaigns.
3. Pressure younger generations to become more active in government-led activities (e.g., German Youth), and over time (years), the process of withering away Church support will drop to acceptable levels.
4. Create differences between East German youth and older generations on their views of the Church.
5. Spread misinformation (lies) about pastors from various Churches in an effort to effectively turn against one another and Church policy.
6. Pressure pastors to become politically loyal to the socialist cause and in return, promise them concessions (breaks) to define the Church cause and directions.
7. Use blackmail (false information) to pressure selected pastors to stepdown.

8. Block acceptance to higher education or expel students who either are not active in the Free German Youth (club for young socialists) or dedicated Socialist party members.
9. Require all youth to be confirmed (accepted into) the *Jugendweihe*, which represents loyalty to the socialist government.

As a high ranking member of the MfS, please answer the following questions. Please be ready to defend your decisions.
1. Which two proposed actions do you believe most effective in decreasing the growing Church influence? Why?
2. Which two proposed actions do you believe to be the most unrealistic and least effective in controlling the Church's influence?
3. When, if ever, does the government have the right to control or influence organizations that directly influences its citizens? Are there exceptions?
4. Of the potential concerns expressed by the East German government about Church threats, which do you believe is most harmful? Least harmful?

Antigovernment Activities: What Would You Do?—Forced-Choice Lesson

Miriam Mundt, age eighteen years, was an art student at Leipzig University. Miriam's family had no reported files for "anti-Socialist" activities. Mundt was initially brought to Stasi office #459 when she and others were photographed partaking in "suspicious" activities involving Western artists displaying works at the State-sponsored "EAST/WEST Art Show." Several students indicated Mundt's willingness to "express her ideas" against the socialist state. On 11 February, Dr. Helms Guerring, Mundt's art professor, was questioned about her anti-government propaganda for forty-eight hours. After the interview, the professor listed Mundt and three friends as "possibly enacting on their beliefs." The professor was encouraged not to talk about his questioning. On 17 February 1963, Miriam Mundt along with Engrid Schmidt made and distributed pamphlets to speak out and against local party (Government) reforms on culture and safety. Both women allegedly pasted home-made pamphlets at the main train station in Leipzig in an effort to distribute their beliefs. Local Volkspolizie (Police) questioned several individuals. Miriam, on 18 February, gave two pamphlets to Peter Hans, a former schoolmate. Christopher Hans, Peter's father, is an active member in the ruling SED and turned the evidence over to Stasi station #495 in Leipzig. On 19 February while Miriam Mundt was attending class, Agents HN 003, HN 328, and HN 761 entered her apartment. The investigation indicated the following items:
1. Western magazines and newspapers
2. Several Western music records
3. Red rubber letters used in a printing press (most were cut or destroyed)

As the District Director for the Ministry for State Security, you have several options or actions that you may choose in this situation. The evidence suggests that Miriam and her friends are active enemies against the East German government and people. Since you are the District Director, you have the final decision in this matter. Now, what do you do? Please examine the following actions:
1. Continue surveillance on Miriam and her friends. Conduct "shadow surveillance," that is, follow the women without being seen until agents find quality evidence supporting antigovernment.
2. Influence Miriam's art professor to fail her. Doing so might distance her from such antigovernment activities.
3. Recruit IMs in her class to report any activity regarding Miriam and her friends.
4. Increase surveillance at the "EAST/WEST Art Show" to gain additional information on Miriam and others.
5. Stop the "EAST/WEST Art Show" all together. Doing so takes away potentially negative influences.

6. "Bug" Miriam's apartment with tiny listening devices to gather information.
7. Monitor all telephone activity from Miriam's house. Information gathered may lead to additional monitoring of others.
8. Collect sensitive and secret information about Miriam and then spread rumors, effectively ruining her reputation.
9. Arrest Miriam based on the evidence given. Use sleep deprivation until additional information is gathered.
10. Drop all surveillance and move to another case.

Members of your group are to agree on *one* of the above options. You should have some basis for agreement. You must make every attempt to reach a common conclusion that all are willing to accept and support.

The three possible actions (in no particular order) taken by the District Director for Stasi operations are:
1.
2.
3.

Of the three possible actions listed above, the best is:

Discussion Starters:
1. If Miriam's family were active members in the government, would it change your decision? Why? Why not?
2. When, if ever, does the government have the right to gather information on citizens?

Demoralization Measures—Persisting Issues Lesson

Directions: As a newly assigned office for the Ministry for State Security (MfS), you have been given a book describing how to "demoralize" the enemy. In this case, the enemy is any fellow East German who has been labeled as hostile toward the communist government. Read the following measure (guideline) issued by your government and then decide which method is most and least effective.

Demoralization measures are designed to provoke, take advantage of and reinforce contradictions and/or differences among enemies of the State. Doing so will fragment, paralyze, disorganize, or isolate those who make it their effort to undermine the GDR. Demoralization measures are aimed at groups, organizations and individuals and use a variety of "independent" methods to ensure success. Such measures should be used when there is necessary evidence available for a crime against the State. Proven methods of demoralization are:

1. Systematic (continued) discrediting of an individual's public reputation and self-esteem on the basis of untrue information(s) that may be combined to damage an individual's credibility. For example: Publicly announce that the suspected individual is actively working for the Stasi, effectively ruining any trust and credibility from the public.
2. Systematic organization of professional (job-related) and social failures (reputation among peers outside of work) for the purpose of destroying the self-confidence of an individual. For example: Providing false information about drinking and drug problems to an individual's employer and then suggest that fellow workers have provided support for such habits.
3. Purposefully undermining an individual's image of role models (e.g., employers, family, pastors) by false information to create doubt about the particular role model's honesty. For example: Place things such as drugs on a suspected individual's parent to destroy any established trust between the two subjects.
4. Creation of mistrust and mutual suspicion within groups and organizations. For example: Create controversy in the suspected individual's church by providing contradicting information about various members of the church.
5. Creation and/or use of reinforcement of rivalries within groups or organizations by taking advantage of individual's emotions. For example: Provide the proper documentation and publicity for two famous "underground bands" to both play at a popular spring concert. At the last moment, revoke the privileges of one band to cause hatred among band members and fans, and then spread false rumors about each band.
6. Infiltrate potential hostile-negative groups and take advantage of potential internal problems. For example: Infiltrate and become a member of a group of writers and artists. At certain planned events, create situations of doubt or unrest to hinder the groups cause.

7. Restrict groups from organizing based on legal and valid regulations. For example: All religious group activities are not allowed on "gather" outside or off church grounds.

Which of the following methods of demoralization do you believe to be most effective?

Which of the following methods of demoralization do you believe to be least effective?

Do you believe such "demoralization measures" serve a purpose in society?

When, if ever, is it appropriate for an organization to actively demoralize another individual or organization?

Do you believe "demoralization" takes place at your school by either teachers, students, or administrators?

FOUR

THE BERLIN WALL: DIVIDE AND RULE

THE WEST BERLIN DILEMMA

In the 1950s, Socialist Unity Party (SED) officials were growing concerned with the permanent departure of East Berliners to West Berlin. It was estimated that between 100,000 and 150,000 East Berliners simply crossed the imaginary border between East and West Berlin never to return each year, effectively draining the GDR of both talented and skilled workers and their income. West Berlin served as a serious economic threat to both East Berlin and the GDR (Fritz 2009). While an estimated 12,000 to 13,000 West Berliners worked in East Berlin, nearly 57,000 East Germans worked in and smuggled goods to West Berlin daily to serve West Germany's consumer needs. In the eyes of the communist government, East Berliners escaping and even working in West Berlin were economic nightmares. East Germans working in West Berlin slowly drained the GDR's socialized healthcare system and education. Supporting the lost tax revenues of East Germans working in West Berlin and receiving government subsidies cost the GDR an estimated one billion dollars a year. In all, some 1.6 million skilled East Germans left the GDR via West Berlin, creating a vacuum of skilled labor before the construction of the first-generation wall (made of barbed wire, concrete blocks, and fences) was constructed in August 1961.

On Sunday 13 August 1961, under the direction of the SED, 10,000 armed East German border guards began closing the border (street), river crossings, as well as selected train stations and communications to West. Four weeks after the barbed wire was erected, the SED authorized the use of border troops to be permanently stationed for the protection of East Berlin. Such border troops were a part of the army that fell under the authority of the Defense Ministry and received battle tanks, machine guns, and weapons of war in an effort to intimidate East Berliners. Motivation of border guards wasn't an easy task. Once a border guard realized the pending invasion from the West was a myth and the newly constructed wall was to hold East Berliners in rather than West Berliners out, moral was often considered low. In an effort to combat low morale and maintain a proper defense readiness, border guards received "ideological encouragement" from the government in addition to specially placed Stasi agents acting as border guards (Flemming 2009).

Life by the Berlin Wall

At the completion of the first generation of the Berlin Wall, it was estimated that nearly 120,000 East Germans lived or worked by the evolving wall. In an effort to maintain security and control without the total domination of border guards, the GDR created "volunteer helpers" to check passes for the border zone. Such special passes, often referred to as "green passes" or even "grave tickets," allowed specially authorized East Germans the opportunity to work and live within the confides of the Wall. Such volunteer helpers were the civilian equivalent to military border guards. While Stasi operations and unofficial informers (IMs) were successful in infiltrating escape groups, volunteer helpers were seen as civilian protectors of the GDR. Assigned to patrol selected areas along the Wall and track down suspicious East Germans, the volunteer helpers were effective in deterring escapes. They were often tasked to (1) seek out suspicious individuals and arrest border violators, (2) control traffic at critical border crossings, (3) safeguard important factories and property deemed as important to the GDR, and (4) aide in searching for border violators who have broken security. Between the years 1974 and 1979, volunteer helpers successfully deterred over 4,000 East Germans before they made it to the first series of fences along the Berlin Wall (Flemming 2009).

For those who lived near the border zone, life could be rather stressful. For those who obtained permission to live and work in the border zone, enduring illuminated lights at night and border patrols served as a constant reminder that they were sealed off from the Western world. However, living by the Wall had its advantages. Families living by the Wall were often well supplied with the latest goods due to the increased military presence (supplying individuals working in the border zone) and the propaganda images of communism for the West (Turner 1987).

Escape Operations

For those desperate enough to risk possible death or imprisonment, the idea of escaping East Berlin was both a dream and reality. In its earliest form, the Berlin Wall consisted of barbed wire and concrete blocks. Escaping by creeping under the barbed wire, climbing over the Wall, or even ramming fortifications with a vehicle quickly came to an end. In reality, most if not all who tried to escape failed. According to border guard reports, of the 4,596 known escape attempts, 3,984 or 87% failed to reach the first barrier (Flemming 2009). Because of this, tunnel operations were the most common method of escape. Since the sewage and water systems were sealed off with thorough welds of all manhole covers, the tunnel method was dangerous. Unlike portrayed in movies and stories, only a few individuals escaped alone during the early years of Wall construction. Professional "helpers" had more reliable and simpler methods of escape through vehicles or foreign passports. While it would seem that escape by car would be the logical selection for escape, failed attempts provided both border guards and

Stasi agents detailed examples of things like hidden compartments, used to intensify control of the border. In the end, most escapes failed (see Table 4.1).

Table 4.1 Selected Examples of Failed Escapes (1961–1989)

Attempted method of escape	Total deaths
Jumping from building into border area	4
Shot or drowned while swimming	22
Shot escaping from train or vehicle	4
Shot escaping through tunnel	2
Shot running through or over border area	32
Shot before border area	3

Source: Strasse 2007.

The Ministry for State Security (MfS) effectively infiltrated agents and IMs into escape groups and their helpers. Captured helpers and alleged escapees faced years of imprisonment, and information gained through creative interrogation techniques provided detailed future escapes and tactics, creating almost a "cause and effect" reaction. The end result led to the second- and third-generation construction and fortification of the Berlin Wall, which added various obstacles along the border zone. In the mid-1970s, the SED ordered the construction of a new wall. Such a wall was designed largely impart for psychological representation from the imperialist West and also from the numerous failed escape attempts by East Germans. Known as "Wall 75," the newer construction added concrete segments in the ground to provide both stability and a greater detection for those attempting to crawl under the Wall. The most dramatic upgrade was a series of concrete pipes or tubes placed at the top of the outer wall to ensure greater difficulty in gaining leverage and climbing. Additional reinforcements were designed for the greatest protection from escape. Wall 75 consisted of eight obstacles, each strategically placed to detect fugitives. Such obstacles encountered (from first to last) were: (1) a concrete wall, (2) chain link signal fence with alarms, (3) grated sand trap area with barbed wire and spikes, (4) observation towers, (5) industrial street lights, (6) cross-country routes used by guard dogs, roaming motorcycle patrols, and border guards, (7) antivehicle ditch constructed of concrete, and (8) concrete wall with tubing. The guarding and protection of the border zone included permanent roaming patrols of two-man border soldiers placed at irregular intervals to confuse fugitives, along with dog patrols and motorcycles (Burnett 2007; Flemming 2009).

LESSONS AND ACTIVITIES

The following lessons are designed to reinforce materials found in this chapter in partnership with the school-adopted content textbook. The following lessons should be used as supplemental text and lessons in an effort to increase cognition over issues associated with the Berlin Wall. With this in mind, multiple styles of lessons and levels of learning are provided, each covering material related to various issues associated with border and escape operations. Lesson One, "Escape from Berlin," is a content-centered, rank-order lesson that provides students with a series of possible escape options from East Berlin. Lesson Two, "Escape from Berlin," is a simulation designed to encourage students' creativity and resourcefulness in an attempt to escape from East Berlin without detection from Stasi agents. Lesson Three, "Heinrich Lummer: East German Border Guard," is a content-centered, forced-choice lesson that places students in an ethical dilemma faced by border guard officers.

Escape from Berlin—Rank-Order Lesson

Your Dilemma: The date is 15 May 1964. You and your friends are citizens in the GDR (East Germany). However, there is nothing "democratic" about the oppressive communist government. Since your country was freed in 1948 from Russian occupation, your government has become increasingly paranoid about its labor force leaving for the West. The Berlin Wall has significantly reduced your fellow East Germans from traveling to West Berlin. The East German secret police (Stasi) are ruthless in both spying on the citizens of East Germany, but also in how they "obtain" information. Stasi infiltration into every aspect of East German life is guaranteed.

The communist "planned economy" in which you live is marginal at best compared to your fellow Germans living in West Berlin. Often, when you and your friends walk beside the fortified wall separating the two cities, you can hear and see the fast-paced lifestyles of West Berlin. This sense of freedom, along with recent arrests of several friends by the Stasi, has only fueled your desires to escape to a better life. With this desire also comes fear. Since the Wall's initial construction in 1961, over thirty East Germans have died trying to escape. It has been rumored that some have escaped while others who are caught simply disappear. Successfully escaping is a good thing, but it will come with consequences. When and if you and your friends escape to West Berlin, the Stasi and other government officials will act swiftly when you fail to report to your assigned jobs the following day. Most likely your family will be arrested, along with other friends not directly associated with your escape.

Earlier this morning, you had a brief opportunity to "peek" at a folder with top secret Stasi documents. Consider this a rare gift. The Stasi agent who carelessly left this material unattended will pay for his mistakes later. State police are aware of the situation but do not know if anyone has actually examined the documents. Later that evening, you and your friends sit down in your apartment to discuss possible escape scenarios.

Possible Choices: Which of the following escape plans does your group believe are the most realistic and least realistic in an effort to escape to West Berlin?

- **Option A:** With scrap metal and a motorcycle engine, build a small ultra light–style aircraft. Practice will not be possible, so mark your aircraft with Russian markings. It is believed a GDR border guard will not fire upon a Soviet aircraft.
- **Option B:** Using sewage access cover (manholes), you could attempt to escape through the elaborate sewage system that connects West Berlin. At designated "choke" points throughout the sewage system are welded bars similar to those found in prisons.
- **Option C:** Build a hot air balloon from scrap parts and by piecing together bits of nylon and bed sheets to make a frighteningly fragile escape. Gas burners from your apartments will act as engines.
- **Option D:** Steal a Russian-built, East German armored vehicle and drive it into the Wall.
- **Option E:** Drive a stolen delivery truck at full speed into wall fortifications, and then attempt to climb electric fence using deflated rubber inner tubes.
- **Option F:** Use an inflatable mattress and attempt to swim one of the canals or rivers at night in an attempt to avoid East German patrols.
- **Option G:** Attempt to gather materials and make (as closely as possible) East German border guard uniforms. Making correct identification papers will be almost impossible. Take a GDR soldier hostage and attempt to escape through one of the eight checkpoints with West Berlin.
- **Option H:** Steal a State-owned bus and attempt to smash it into wall fortifications, and then attempt to climb electric fence using deflated rubber inner tubes.
- **Option I:** Dig a tunnel to escape. Water tables (amount of water found in the soil) are generally high. Because of this, GDR border guards sporadically check buildings and ground for tunneling activities.
- **Option J:** Other—Your group develops a plan of escape.

Decision Sheet: Below, your group will assign a rank (order) of the most to the least realistic methods of escape. With each ranking, your group is asked to provide a potential positive and negative factor(s) for each potential escape.

Assigned Rank (e.g., 1, 2)	Type of Option Given	Potential Positive Factor(s)	Potential Negative Factor(s)
	A: Glider		
	B: Sewage escape		
	C: Hot air balloon		
	D: Armored vehicle		
	E: Delivery truck		
	F: Inflatable mattress		
	G: Hostage situation		
	H: Bus		
	I: Tunnel		
	J: Other		

Which escape plan does your group believe is *least* likely to succeed?

Which escape plan does your group believe is *most* likely to succeed?

Escape from Berlin—Simulation

Goals: Given a simulation designed to provide students with insights into the working of a totalitarian society and the ruthless and oppressive brutality of a police state, this simulation is designed for students to better <u>understand</u> the difficulties involved in escaping from East Berlin through air, ground, or water.

Objectives: Given the opportunity, students will be able to:
1. Investigate documented escape attempts.
2. Analyze various methods of escape via water, air, and ground.
3. Construct a detailed escape plan.
4. Present escape plan to class.

Procedure: Teacher
1. Before one begins the "Escape from Berlin" activity, attempt to decorate the room in East German and Soviet flags and posters made by students. Nuclear survival guides, propaganda posters and pictures of the period and historical readings and/or lectures are helpful in terms of background information.
2. Decide how you will divide student into teams. Before groups are formed, predetermine select students that will act as Stasi agents and provide you with valuable escape attempt information. Such student's identity status will remain secret.
3. Once students have either been placed into groups or allowed to select their own (preferred), provide each group with the simulation instructions for students and grading rubric. Carefully go through each document and check for understanding.

Procedure: Students
1. Once your group has been organized, carefully review the project guidelines and scoring criteria. After doing so, each student within the group should select a job title from a list developed by your teacher.
2. Once you begin to design an escape plan, your group may purchase hard-to-find items through the black market (your teacher). Your teacher will determine the amount of money each group will receive. Purchasing difficult to find items will allow your group the opportunity to discuss your escape plan with the teacher – who will remain neutral throughout the simulation.
3. In an effort to make the possibility of obtaining hard-to-find items, your teacher will determine given material through a coin toss. If the coin toss ruled against the purchase of the required goods, the group will have to abandon their plan.
4. The Stasi or East German Secret Police will also be present. It is recommended you keep your plans a secret. If you hear other groups' plans, you may become an IM for the teacher.

5. You are NOT allowed to provide information on your OWN group.
6. You will make a detailed presentation of your escape plan to your peers. After all presentations, groups will then vote on the most realistic and probable plan of escape. Groups are not allowed to vote for their own escape plan.

Escape from East Berlin—Student Handout/Instructions

Time warp! You wake up to find that your group had been transformed into East Germans trapped behind the Berlin Wall in the year 1987. Your four to five member groups must escape. Your first step is organization. Security is critical. There are undercover members of the Stasi or secret police in this room. They will be rewarded if they "spy" on your escape plans. No person in your group can inform on your own group, but assume that other groups have "Stasi" in them. Your group will need to fill the following escape plan positions:

A. You will need to elect a *coordinator*. For security, this is the sole person who can talk to other groups or contact the black market.
B. A *researcher* is critical. Map-reading and ability to successfully tap into the correct computer databases is vital. There can be more than one researcher in a group.
C. *Readers* must be present for the group presentation to the class. They must also read out the agreed answers to the coordinated plan. All members of your resistance group can help the reader answer questions during the presentation.
D. *Writers* must have either sufficient typing skills or legible handwriting and the ability to transcribe verbal information with accuracy. The ability to draw or draft plans can be a plus.

Your group must come up with an example of each of the three methods of escape. There are *over, under,* and *through*. You need to concentrate on the pan that you decide to use. You must briefly mention the two categories of escape methods that your group contemplated but didn't select. Diagrams, maps, and handouts should be used.

Security is paramount! Here, it can impact your grade. In reality, you could be sent to jail or be barred from higher education or a respectable job in the workplace. Every time you talk to the black market, you must have a written record of our escape needs on your black market contact sheet. Turn in the sheet attached to your plan.

Your teacher is a neutral figure in this simulation. He/she is also someone your group can call upon for advice without fear of compromised security. They will tell you what can be purchased on black market versus what you can legally obtain on the open market. Any materials that need to be purchased on the black market are decided on a coin toss. If you lose the toss, you forfeit that particular plan and must design another. If you lose four coin tosses, your group will receive your first initial choice.

The black marketer is an illegal but somewhat tolerated part of the planned economy. The Volkspolizie (police) probably know who the person is, so expect them to take no chances on your behalf. Your coin toss simulates the reality that the marketer might turn you in to stay in good graces with authorities. His or her life is on the line even if your group is successful. Attempt to purchase weapons, and the black marketer will turn you in!

Remember that by escaping, you will put your family in danger. They, most likely, will be punished, and you will surely never see them as long as the communist government remains in power.

Grading Rubric for Students

	Points
Written Grading Guide	
1st plan you didn't use and why. Length: One paragraph.	10
2nd plan you didn't use and why. Length: One paragraph.	10
3rd plan in detail. Length: Two pages minimum.	40
Security not broken. (Stasi agents obtain information.)	10
Black market paperwork.	10
Quality of writing (punctuation, grammar, etc.)	20
Verbal Grading Guide	
1st plan you didn't use and why. Length: One minute.	10
2nd plan you didn't use and why. Length: One minute.	10
3rd plan in detail. Length: Five to eight minutes.	40
Security not broken (Stasi agents informing class of plans)	15
Answering questions from audience	10
Visual aids.	10
Coordination of group effort.	5
Total	200

10-point security bonus for turning in <u>accurate</u> written plans of other groups.

Heinrich Lummer: East German Border Guard—Forced-Choice Lesson

Heinrich Lummer was nineteen-years-old when he was told to enter the East German army "in an effort to serve the socialist agenda of the East German people." Raised in East Berlin, Heinrich privately hated the socialist government and "wall of oppression" between East and West Berlin. However, in fear of the government's harsh treatment of those who questioned the government and possible Stasi spies within his unit, he was reluctant to express his disgust. Assigned to the northern sector of the Berlin Wall, Heinrich regularly witnessed civilian brutality at the hands of East German border guards. One summer night, while on patrol, Heinrich tossed a note in an empty bottle over the Wall to the West Berlin sector. In the note, Heinrich anonymously described in detail his hatred for the Wall, the socialist government, and the Soviet Union's presence in East Germany. Three days later, a West German news radio station read Heinrich's anonymous letter to their Western audience in an effort to document the oppression of the East German people. Three weeks after the radio broadcast, while working in his border guard unit's barracks, Heinrich and several others were arrested by three Stasi agents. It was noted at his arrest that a Stasi spy working for the West Berlin radio station had copied the note and, through military records, traced the note to his unit. Heinrich and ten fellow border guards were charged with espionage and transported to the hated Brandenburg prison.

As a high ranking member of the Stasi, you must *individually* select one of the following actions. Please consider the nature of the crime against the East German people and how to prevent similar future situation found above.

1. Deprive Heinrich of food and water for an extended period of time until he confesses to crimes against the socialist state. Make him serve ten to fifteen years of hard labor.
2. Arrest Heinrich's family and charge them with "failure to report crimes against the State." Make an example of Heinrich's mother with a year-long sentence of hard labor.
3. Reward the Stasi spy working at the West German news radio station with a promotion and increase incentives to expose border guards who he *suspects* of antigovernment activities.
4. Isolate Heinrich's officer in charge of his unit until he gives a confession. Once a confession is made, execute him for treason against the people and not properly controlling his unit. Rotate guards on patrol each evening to promote distrust and fear to conduct such antigovernment activities.
5. Reassign all members of Heinrich's unit to remote locations throughout East Germany.
6. Force confessions from several of Heinrich's unit. Each confession will be followed by two years of hard labor.

7. Increase electronic surveillance on all guards patrolling the Berlin Wall.
8. Secretly assign Stasi agents to each border guard unit. All suspicious activity will be reported and *suspected* guards will be reassigned or jailed.
9. Imprison Heinrich for life, making an example to fellow border guard units of the harsh punishment for espionage activities against the East German people/state. Rotate guards on patrol each evening in an effort to promote distrust and fear to conduct such antigovernment activities.

As a group, you must agree on *one* of the above options offered. As a group, you should seek some basis for agreement. The group must make every attempt to reach a common conclusion to protect the Socialist State of East Germany.

The three possible actions taken by the Stasi were narrowed down to:
1.
2.
3.

Of the three decisions listed above, the best is:

Discussion Starters

1. Is it correct for a government to spy on its own citizens? Try to give an example of when it's appropriate and when it's not appropriate.
2. Suppose you were in charge of the West Berlin radio station. Would you have read the letter knowing there was a possibility of a Stasi crackdown?
3. Do you believe Heinrich's open questioning of his government's political policies and his actions is espionage?

FIVE

BECOMING A GOOD SOCIALIST: YOUTH AND EDUCATION

THE EAST GERMAN EDUCATIONAL SYSTEM

The Socialist Unity Party (SED) believed the East German youth were the future of East Germany. In an effort to guarantee its political survival, the SED played an active role as early as 1946 to mold the educational process in its political and social favor. East Germany youth were viewed as the "collective good" through the eyes of Communist party, and such educational reform emphasis of community and society would be bigger than any individual by identifying and grooming future Communist party members at the tender age of six-years-old (Fulbrook 2005). Yet even before students were exposed to communist ideology at school, children attending preschool experienced the concept of togetherness. According to Rŭckel (2008), in an effort to stop children from using large amounts of diapers and unnecessary trips to the potty, nursery workers would take the entire class to the bathroom (potty) at the same time. All students remained on the "potty" until everyone was finished. Why? Such actions were two-fold: (1) It saved on the usage of diapers, and (2) It illustrated the need for community/team rather than individualism. This unofficial step in the education system was every child's introduction to the sense of community and merely a precursor before entering grade school.

The first stage in becoming a "good socialist" was to become a member of Young Pioneers. At age six, the Young Pioneers wore blue neckerchiefs and were taught primarily through cartoons and music. Young Pioneers were taught how to organize charity events for other socialist countries and campaigns and how to raise money to improve their school. Becoming a Thalmann Pioneer was the second step that was distinguishable by students who wore a red neckerchief. Thälmann Pioneers were nine years of age when they began attending carefully orchestrated socialist activities and propaganda through music, fitness, art, and books. The third and final step to develop socialist youth was the joining of Free German Youth. Students and young adults from ages fourteen to twenty-five were encouraged to embrace the Socialist party (Hansel 2004; Fritz 2009; Watts 1994).

Students who joined the Free German Youth (FDJ) were encouraged to accept and be initiated in the socialist tradition of Jugendweihe, which transformed fourteen- and fifteen-year-olds into adults. Designed to mirror religious rituals such as the Catholic Communion, Protestant Confirmation, or Jewish Bar Mitzvah, the Jugendweihe rejected the notion of religion and based decisions on science, logic, and society (Lottich 1963; Fritz 2009). However, before the Jugendweihe ritual could take place, students were required to demonstrate a general working knowledge of the socialist system and the working class through a series of events and themes (see Table 5.1). Becoming a member of the FDJ had its privileges. The FDJ was responsible for most of the nation's youth groups, festivals, concerts, and social clubs in efforts to reach and maintain the East German youth in the Marxist-Leninist philosophy of communism (Diefendorf 1982).

Table 5.1 Example of Organized Events for Jugendweihe

Theme 1: Socialism—Our World Event 1: The Time in Which We Live Event 2: What People Have Created Belongs to the People Event 3: We Are This State *Theme 2: What Does It Mean to Be Revolutionary Today?* Event 1: To Learn From the Soviet Union, Means to Learn How to Win Event 2: Your Work, Your Responsibility, Your Honor Event 3: You Need the Socialist Society – the Socialist Society Needs You Event 4: Courage and Heroism in Our Time Event 5: To Recognize True Beauty and Experience Culture *Theme 3: On the Path to a Happy Future* Event 1: We Understand the World and Change Things Event 2: We are Prepared for the Communist Tomorrow

Source: Fritz 2009.

With the small exception of youth whose parents were active members of the SED, most students joined simply because of the activities and privileges granted to members. As a member of the FDJ, youth were more likely to find employment or attend college after completing the State's minimum of ten years of compulsory education, in which party membership was often required. The East German school system was mandatory to age fourteen. Ten years of regulated school earned students a diploma from the Polytechnic High School (POS). Students wishing to pursue additional training and education could select from a variety of options. The Extended High School (EOS) was an additional level of specialized education (e.g., farming, masonry). Apprenticeship training is another three-year, two-way "hands-on" learning after POS. Technical college in the forms of medical-pedagogical and technical-economic was awarded to students after three years of study beyond POS. Technical degrees were associated with general medical training, training for teachers, and training for those seeking professions such as engineering without a diploma. Lastly, students seeking degrees (with diploma) attended a State-controlled university for five years (Rückel 2008, 35). Regardless of the education obtained, the goals were full employment and to provide a modest income for one's family. In the GDR, work was considered the most important aspect of life. Much like in the United States, individuals had his/her area of expertise based on experience and education (see Table 5.2).

Table 5.2 Example of Education, Job Title, and Salary

Position	Education	Salary (monthly)
Sales clerk	POS + 2 ½ years training	600–800
Bricklayer	POS + 2 years training	1,110–1,370
Chemist	EOS + University	1,000–1,300
Farmer	POS + 2 years training	1,197
Prof. engineer	POS + Technical College 2–3 years or EOS and University	1,470
Mine worker	POS + 3 years training	1,167–1,444

Source: Rückel 2008.

LESSONS AND ACTIVITIES

The following lessons are designed to reinforce materials found in this chapter in partnership with the school-adopted content textbook. The following lesson should be used as supplemental text and lessons in an effort to increase cognition over issues associated with the youth and education. With this in mind, multiple styles of lessons and levels of learning are provided, each covering content material related to various issues associated with border and escape operations. Lesson One, "Determining Social Responsibility: Political/Social Education or Indoctrination?" is an inductive inquiry lesson designed for students to explore both the guidelines and rules of the Thälmann Pioneers and the vow taken at the Jugendweihe ceremony.

Determining Social Responsibility: Political/Social Education or Indoctrination?—Inductive Inquiry Lesson

For the Teacher.
In society, both students and adults are prescribed sets of rules, guidelines, and standards that a society deems appropriate. This lesson is design to provide students with insight to the East German socialist education system. Students will examine the guidelines for the Thälmann Pioneers that students were required to join during their late elementary to middle grade school education and later were to examine the pledge taken during the Jugendweihe ceremony given at ages fourteen and fifteen years to youth wishing to join the socialist society. The desired goal of this lesson is not to suggest that either guideline or ceremony is acceptable but rather to have students think about how society places guidelines, norms, etc. on its citizens. Whether it is through a political, religious, or school environment, how does one truly determine social responsibility? Does society or institutions favor agendas over others?

Step 1: A question is raised and stated clearly.
Ask the class if they have ever been given an oath or a set of guidelines or rules in order to receive something. Do you believe society (e.g., government, school, religious organizations) has an agenda to maintain social responsibility? Or do you believe such institutions provide such guidelines, rules, etc. in efforts to indoctrinate into social norms?

Step 2: A tentative answer is developed.
Encourage the class to explore the question(s) provided in Step 1. On the board, ask students to brainstorm of various events/times in their lives where either a set of rules or oaths are given to establish a lifestyle. This may include the Boy Scouts, Girl Scouts, Catholic Communion, Protestant Confirmation, Jewish Bar Mitzvah, etc. What made such events/times in their lives so important? Ask students if there are situations where such events/times would not be appropriate? For example, some East German parents didn't necessarily approve of the Young Pioneers, the Thälmann Pioneers, or even the Free German Youth because they went against their religious or personal beliefs. While considered the minority, these East Germans viewed such activities as a form of political and social indoctrination by the socialist government.

Step 3: Evidence bearing on the tentative answer is gathered.
Either individually or in small groups, provide students with the handout titled, "The Laws of the Thälmann Pioneers" and "Taking the Vow: The Jugendweihe Ceremony." Ask the students to brainstorm of potential strengths, weaknesses, and potential concerns of accepting and following such actions? Do they believe these are forms of social responsibility (i.e., designed to better society)? Or are these potential forms of political and social indoctrination? What, if any, sepa-

rates these examples from traditional oaths, social or religious events, or rules from these two examples?

Step 4: A conclusion is drawn from the evidence.
Have individual students or small groups present their findings either in writing or to the class. Ask students to discuss the similarities and differences between today's society and that of socialist East German society.

Step 5: Conclusion is applied to the original question(s).
On the board, conduct a class discussion over student findings. Provide students with information found in chapter five.

The Laws of the Thälmann Pioneers

Ernst Thälmann was an important historical figure in East German society. Leader of the German Communist Party in 1925, he was imprisoned and killed by the Nazis in 1944. To honor his accomplishments, students leaving the Young Pioneers were promoted to the Thälmann Pioneers to help them become better citizens. After a short ceremony, students (ages ranging from nine to thirteen years) were given the following guidelines on how to behave as Thälmann Pioneers:

We Thälmann Pioneers love our socialist fatherland, the German Democratic Republic. With words and action, we will always and everywhere side with our State, which is an integral part of the community of socialist states.

We wear our red neckerchief with pride and treat it with respect. Our red neckerchief represents the working class's flag, and it's a great honor to wear it as a sign of our close ties with the cause of the working class and its party.

We love and respect our parents. We know that we owe our parents much. We follow their advice and help them always. We want to become conscious creators of the socialist society.

We love and protect peace and hate war. We strengthen socialism and help peace-loving forces all over the world by learning diligently and doing good deeds. We will face always and everywhere the lives of others.

We are friends of the Soviet Union and of all socialist countries and maintain friendships with all children in the world.

The friendship with the Soviet Union is important to us. The Lenin Pioneers are our best friends.

We acquire thorough knowledge and skills and stand up for tidiness, discipline, and cleanliness. We encourage everyone to learn without cheating, to use their knowledge, and to make sure that words match action. This way, we prepare for life and work in the socialist society.

We love to work and respect work and all working people. We learn from workers, farmers, and other members of the working population, and we lend a hand wherever help is needed. We protect public property.

We love the truth, are reliable, and are friends with each other. We always seek the truth and stand up for socialism. We accomplish assigned tasks and give our word of honor as Pioneers. We ensure that our Pioneer group will become a team of comrades, and we will help our fellow students.

We make ourselves familiar with engineering, the study of laws of nature, and our cultural treasures. We are interested in the latest developments in science and technology.

We Thälmann Pioneers keep our bodies clean and healthy, regularly take part in sports, and are cheerful.

Taking the Vow: The Jugendweihe Ceremony

The Jugendweihe was an initiation and celebration of youth entering adulthood and the socialist society. Generally, students were between the ages of fourteen and fifteen years when they took part in the Jugendweihe ceremony. However, before the ceremony could take place, students had to illustrate their knowledge of socialism through a series of events where students must do research, visit locations, and demonstrate a thorough knowledge of the socialist system. As students began their collective entry into an auditorium, the director of the ceremony said:

Dear Young Friends,

Are you, as young citizens of the German Democratic Republic, prepared to work and fight for the great and noble case of socialism and to honor the revolutionary heritage of our people? If so, please answer, "Yes, we do!"

Are you, as devoted sons and daughters of our workers' and farmers' state, prepared to strive for higher education and culture, to become masters in your field, to learn constantly, and to use all your knowledge and skills for the realization of our great humanistic goals? If so, please answer, "Yes, we do!"

Are you, as worthy members of our socialist society, prepared to work together in a comradely fashion, to base your actions on mutual respect and help, and to always combine the path to your personal happiness with the fight for the happiness of the people? If so, please answer, "Yes, we do!"

Are you, as true patriots, prepared to deepen the strong friendship with the Soviet Union, to strengthen the brotherly ties with the socialist countries, to fight the spirit of wealthy internationalism, and to protect peace and socialism against any capitalist attack? If so, please answer, "Yes, we do!"

We, East Germans, have heard your promise. You have set yourselves a noble target. We welcome you in the society of working people, which in agreement and under the leadership of the working class and its revolutionary party, builds the developed socialist society in the German Democratic Republic.

SIX

THE PLANNED ECONOMY THAT DIDN'T HAVE A PLAN

THE PERILS OF A PLANNED ECONOMY

The East German economy operated on a planned economy concept modeled by the Soviet Union. Due to resistance by the East German government immediately following the Soviet occupation of Eastern Germany after World War II, the collectivization of farms and heavy industry didn't take place until the German Democratic Republic's official formation in October 1949. From this date onward, East German industry followed the strict "heavy" industry model of their Russian occupiers. Across East Germany, steel industries and other forms of heavy manufacturing dotted the landscape. The Socialist Unity Party (SED) indicated the lasting benefits of a planned economy. They believed the radical transformation in society, a plentiful supply of raw material, and strong manufacturing would allow for the government to supply goods and materials to satisfy the needs of East Germany through the planning of production of products and allocation of materials. This socialist goal of satisfying the average needs of the citizen would directly contradict and set it apart from capitalism's needs for profit and exploitation of the working class. As a result, the SED promised, under a planned economy, to supply every East German with basic needs, such as food, clothing, and shelter guaranteed under socialism (Stitziel 2007).

By the late 1950s and early 1960s, the ruling SED began the gradual shift from a heavily planned economy favored by the Soviet Union to a less planned model that incorporated more personal responsibility and limited, State-supported competition with other government-manufactured products. This theory called for products to become sustainable on the market and able to both compete and sell throughout East Germany. Salaries of both workers and supervisors depended largely on the government-based competition among factories. Systemic flaws began to appear within the planned economy model almost immediately after the shift from a heavy industrial base to a structured competition-based design. Such competition among government-controlled companies proved largely unsuccessful. Since all products, retail prices, and supply were controlled by the government, competition among government-owned companies proved hopeless. Furthermore, supplying the East German population with the basic needs (e.g., food, clothing, shelter) naturally transformed into higher needs among the population. Luxury items besides the basic needs in society were not considered necessary under the doctrine of socialism, and such luxury needs would be logistically impossible to produce and distribute among East German citizens (Rŭckel 2008).

A Planned Economy

The rationale for cheap and affordable prices for the basic needs in East German citizens resonated with most socialist politicians. It was these politicians that grew up under the previous German capitalist governments and who lived in poor conditions with limited amounts of food, supplies, and financial hardship. The opportunity to establish a fixed pricing policy guaranteed every citizen in the GDR affordable prices for the required basic needs in society. Such prices of goods and the amount of production and distribution would be fixed by the socialist government's Office of Prices after careful planning and consideration by the Politburo. With the extreme exception of farmers produce, prices for products cost the same throughout East Germany, whether they sold or not. The issue of supply and demand created logistical issues for government-controlled companies operating in East Germany. Products that would stay on store shelves in West Germany for weeks or months would rarely stay on East German store shelves for one hour. This rapid consumption of East German products was not due to their quality or taste; rather, such demand was created for goods because of the inconsistency of daily and weekly deliveries of goods from State-controlled factories. As a result, families often stockpiled selected products and saved them due to the uncertainty of availability. Fitz (2009), illustrates a popular East joke that illustrates the daily shortages of everyday supplies. "A man walks into a store and asks: 'Do you have toilet paper?' The shop assistant replies: 'No, the shop next door is the one where you cannot get toilet paper; we are the shop with no aluminum foil' (103).

Most of the shopkeepers and employees were honest and fair about strategically placing scarce products on shelves throughout the day in efforts to provide those who worked an opportunity to purchase goods. While East Berlin generally received enough goods to marginally meet the demands of consumers, this wasn't the case for areas in rural East Germany. Such areas with smaller populations received unreliable deliveries of goods. Since the importance of goods was often determined by population, the smaller the town, the less priority it had in the eyes of the Office of Prices. In such rural areas, deliveries were once a week on either Tuesday or Wednesday. If deliveries were not made, residents waited until the following week. Certain goods, such as fresh fruits, were difficult to obtain regardless of a city's population or the geographical area.

PLANNING AND PRODUCING GOODS

The East German government followed what was perceived in socialism as the Soviet Union's model of goods production. Centrally, government-controlled five-year plans outlined the general direction of the economy. Such five-year plans were designed to provide a *general* direction of what and how much of any given product should be made. One-year plans were more specific and actually *allocated* material for production of given popular products. An example of this might be shoes. All production costs, to include materials, were based on the previous year's records. Due to the rigid controlled programs of production, materials and production lines couldn't be switched quickly enough from one production to another based on supply and demand. When the population suddenly bought more of one particular product (for example, shoes), there were no additional production facilities or materials allocated to solve the situation due to the pre-allocation of materials. As a result, unplanned and expensive imports of shoes were made by the government with a special note of emphasis to increase the production of shoes as top priority for the next calendar year. Sadly, by this time, consumer purchasing power and type of clothing had shifted to something else. All of the production power and decision-making laid in the hands in East Berlin. As a result, most of the country was stifled both creatively and through production. Manufacturing centers were given a target number of products to manufacture with no other requirements given. Designated companies made a product—nothing more, nothing less. Quality and updated designs were not the top priority, often resulting in very basic goods and traditional patterns of clothing from year to year (Stitziel 2007). The entire process of planning, making, and distributing products often defied consumer wishes on how something was made and where it was sold (see Figure 6.1).

Figure 6.1 Planning, Producing, and Distributing Goods

SED Party Members (Politburo)
↓
Central government (planning committees) determines the overall direction of the economy in terms of orders. Ministry for Trade and Provisioning then determines how many will be produced and who receives the goods.

↓

Fifteen different geographical regions in the GDR enact their "regional interests" under the direction of the Central Government. Orders at this level may have minor changes based on the geographic region needs. Most products are made at this level.
↓
200 districts throughout the country are charged in distribution of selected goods to localities or shops.
↓
Localities sell products to consumers.

ISSUES WITH THE SOCIALIST PLANNED ECONOMY

The old saying "when it rains, it pours" was a true representation of the East German planned economy. The "top-down" approach toward planning what should be produced and the quantity of product created a self-made trap in terms of possible overproduction and surplus. Unlike the capitalist production model that encouraged production based on both supply and demand, the planned production approach operated all factories at full capacity, creating either shortages due to the limited amount of production for the entire country or surpluses from the lack of consumer demand.

Internally, factories attempted to resolve the issue of surpluses and shortages by hording raw materials and labor in efforts to build stockpiles of supplies for future production. This was done on part of the Central Committee's allocation of resources for the entire year. To add to the dilemma was the seemingly lack of quality found in most products. With this in mind, along with the regulation of prices, profits, and amount of goods produced, workers' salaries were often based on the amount of goods produced, leaving little to no incentive for quality. Often, a worker was paid the same if the product was of poor or superior quality, forming ultimately a complacent attitude about production and distribution. To combat this level of despair, East Germans used humor to ease the sometime impoverished conditions. According to Rückel (2008, 43), East Germans used to joke that "everything is available—just not all times and everywhere, especially not when you need it." Indeed, East Germany made high quality goods. East Germany was considered the most developed and industrial member in the Eastern Bloc, second only to the Soviet Union. Even with this recognition, it was not uncommon to find periods when a citizen could not find toilet paper and then the following week could not find pears, apples, or honey. One of the major factors causing such shortages was incorrect delivery to stores and localities and the export of higher quality goods to raise revenues for the SED. The end result to the hit-and-miss supply of goods was East German shoppers who often bought excessive amounts of items in hopes of creating personal surpluses.

The growing concern of surpluses of certain goods caused concern for the government. While fruits, vegetables, desired clothing, and meats were often limited, one of the major factors and causes of surplus was the overwhelming number of goods that sat on shelves for months at a time in certain locations while they were quickly sold in other locations. The theory and strict guidelines and control under a planned economy wouldn't allow for the redistribution of goods from one location to another. Predetermined orders by the Central Government or regional districts were given for each location and region in East Germany. The end result was unsold goods that often added to consumers' anger about the lack of desired items. Products sitting in stores for months only highlighted the dysfunctional elements within the strict planning and guidelines found in the East German and other Eastern Bloc nations' planned economies. For the SED, the simplest and most effective method of eliminating surpluses was to simply reduce the price. The reallocation of goods was not a feasible option. The overall lack of quality and types of goods proved, once again, to be an issue since such products were not desired at the given location. Store managers were encouraged to sell surplus goods regardless of price. In the eyes of the government, it was about volume not price. As a result, the Central Government compensated each store for the reduced price and loss of store revenue during the sale, adding to the inefficiency of the planned economy (Stitziel 2007; Simonovits 1989).

THE SOCIALIST UNITY PARTY'S RATIONALE FOR GOVERNMENT CONTROL OF THE ECONOMY

The SED, from its conception, made it clear that its political and economic survival depended largely on its ability to supply East Germans with not only the basic needs (food, clothing, and shelter) but also a limited supply for those whose desires asked for additional items. This "regulation" of the economy was difficult when West Germany produced goods at an alarming rate. While "state socialism" defined and prided itself as the alternative to capitalism, it shared issues with its class enemy to the West: affluence and a consumers' paradise. However, in reality, many of the modern issues associated with consumption and manufacturing in East Germany came down to the discourse between raw materials, modern manufacturing, consumer consumption, and rigid (often unrealistic) economic policies (see Figure 6.2).

Figure 6.2 Issues Associated with Consumption and Manufacturing

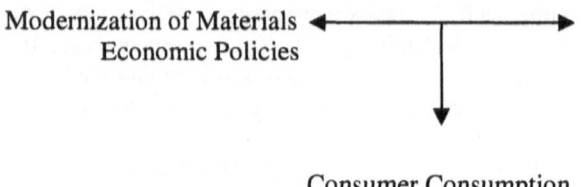

The problem with modernization, increased materials usage, and economic policies proved rather risky for the SED. Since the attempted uprising in 1953 by peasants and workers, the SED was determined to increase the benefits of the working class. In doing so, the SED allowed wages (monthly earnings) to outpace the actual production and productivity and consumption of the consumers' needs. The limited production and selling of more expensive and higher quality goods would, in theory, supplement monies lost by East Germans seeking things beyond the basic needs of society. In economic reality, the SED was relying on those who purchased more expensive and more highly desired goods to artificially inflate workers' salaries and less desirable products, which created a false sense of economic security. Thus, the SED was robbing Peter (those who desired higher quality goods) to pay Paul (inflate the need for lower quality goods), creating the economic problem that plagued all Eastern European economies: What happens when industrial goods don't sell?

To increase their stator as a provider of basic needs, the SED wanted to distinguish between what was considered "real" and "false" needs in society. According to the SED, the needs of the individual are shaped by the social relations of society. The socialist's view toward money equated to the "personal needs" of the people, while the capitalist's view of money equated to "creature comforts" and "social status" (Zatlin 2009). As a result, the SED believed their ideas were superior to those of capitalists because a planned economy removed the grounds of selfish desires by creating social conditions that promoted "real" needs to exist. Denying the power of money and wealth meant, in a communist society, that there would no longer be a societal desire other than government.

In the end, the SED boasted that a planned economy approach was superior to capitalism in a number of ways. First, through government control and regulation, conditions that foster only "real" needs maintained a balanced satisfaction between supply and demand. Second, in communist nations throughout Eastern Europe, every citizen was provided a job through the strict government control and regulation of the markets to provide both stability and control. Third, all citizens in communist nations were protected against poverty. Lastly, in East Germany and other communist nations, the government ensured high social wages through fixed prices (commodities, rent, electricity, water, fuel, etc.) to provide a stable economic system versus an individual's established income (Turner 1987).

Thus, in theory, East German factories should have flourished throughout the country. In reality, the constraints associated with costs (e.g., lack of raw material) resulted in inefficiency, low production and productivity, higher levels of waste, and a general lack of personal incentive to produce quality products or goods, which led to a popular East German quote: "They pretend to pay us, and we pretend to work." Many factories and politicians, to avoid government scrutiny, used "smoke and mirror" techniques to avoid unwanted investigations. For example, when Chairman Honecker demanded to know why East Germans were standing in lines for fresh fruit on his way to work in East Berlin and wanted immediate action, the managers of the store and government officials simply relocated places where citizens could purchase fresh fruit, effectively solving the disheartening view for the Party Chairman! Did it solve the problem of limited quantities of fresh fruit? No. Did it solve Chairman Honecker's anger? Yes.

Producers of State-owned factories found various creative methods to falsify reports on production and output due to shortages of materials while government production targets remained high in efforts to "satisfy" government reports. Such falsified plans of production were done by holding "reserve" resources so they could meet the unrealistic (politician-based) goals established by the SED's Center in Future Plans. Rŭckel (2008) provides an example of unrealistic government goals of production when a director of a porcelain factory told Chairman Honecker that "five percent of our production is rejected," to which Honecker replied "is that enough for the whole country" (46). In fact, many directors simply neglected to report negative news. Most factory directors knew they couldn't fulfill unrealistic plans each year. To avoid criticism, official reports and records of production were sent to the SED when key economic officials were on vacation, effectively avoiding direct confrontation with government officials.

LESSON AND ACTIVITIES

The following lessons are designed to reinforce materials found in this chapter in partnership with the school-adopted content textbook. The following lessons should be used as supplemental text and lessons in an effort to increase cognition over issues associated with the concept of a planned economy. With this in mind, multiple styles of lessons and levels of learning are provided, each covering content material related to perceived strengths and weaknesses of a government-controlled economy. Lesson One, "A Planned Candy Economy," is a simulation lesson that provides students with values a realistic representation of predetermined production and distribution. Lesson Two, "A Central Planned Economy," is a persisting issues lesson designed to illustrate the potential concerns with predetermined allotments of goods while dealing with consumers' needs. Lesson Three, "The Experiment at Central High," is a persisting issues lessons that illustrates the allocation and sell of soda and candy using a planned economic approach. Finally, Lesson Four, "The Bedpan Company: Quality vs. Quantity," is a simulation lesson designed to reinforce documented issues regarding the quality and quantity of government-operated goods versus its capitalist counterparts.

A Planned Candy Economy—Simulation

Goals: Given a simulation designed to provide students with creative insight into the organization and rationale behind a socialist planned economy. This simulation is designed for students to better understand and appreciate the difficulties involved in effectively satisfying consumers' needs while operating on a predetermined budget.

Objectives: Given the opportunity, students will be able to:
1. Compare and contrast the concept of supply and demand and a planned economy.
2. Analyze potential strengths and weaknesses of the planned economy approach.
3. Construct and formulate solutions with supply and demand.

Procedure: Teacher
1. The teacher will need the following items for this simulation:
   a. Individually wrapped pieces of candy
   b. Unsharpened pencils
   c. Enough East German marks (dollars) for all students in the class.
2. Within the class, either select or ask for two volunteers. These two students will be members of the Central Office of Prices. They are representatives observing the markets. They are not allowed to talk to other students.
3. Make space in your classroom for two different stores. These stores may be desks opposite from one another in the classroom. Make one store a school supply material (Schule-Versorgungsmaterial) and the other a candy store (Süßigkeit-Speicher). The school supply store should have pencils available for purchase for 5 marks. Candy should also be available for 5 marks.
4. Ask for a volunteer to work the candy store and a volunteer to work the school supply material.
5. Give each student in the class a total of 10 marks. The two members of the Central Office of Prices will not receive any money.
6. At the teacher's discretion, allow students to freely use their East German marks to purchase the goods they believe are important. Allow for this to take place for a total of three minutes. During this time, ask the two members of the Office of Prices to observe the classroom interactions and purchases without any interaction with their peers purchasing goods.

7. Stop the selling of goods at three minutes. Have students go back to their desks. Ask the two members of the Office of Prices to enter the hallway. Have them determine, based on their observations, which goods should be produced in greater quantities.
8. While the two government officials are outside in the hallway, tell the students the school supply store has a special on pencils. However, this isn't the average pencil—this pencil gives the student ten bonus points on either a homework assignment or a test. Naturally, you are not obligated to honor this claim.
9. Without informing the government members of this conversation, bring in the members from the hallway to observe the next round of purchasing.
10. Allow students to once again purchase goods with their remaining money.

What happens? Do students flock to the school supply store or to the candy store? Odds are that you will see a significant increase of pencil purchases. Ask the two government members what their recommendations were on allotting goods to the public based on their *initial observation*. An overwhelming amount of time, students, acting as government officials, witness the rush to the candy store. This *perceived* demand is thus backed and often supported with the recommendation for more candy to be allocated to the class. In reality, once this official decision is made, the demand for candy *usually* decreases when students are allowed to purchase goods during the second round. The end result is too much candy and not enough pencils. Why?

Explain to the students that the East German government allocated goods, materials, and resources based on the *previous* year's consumption. This was illustrated by the students leaving the classroom after observing the first round of purchases. This planning of future products and goods for production was one important element of a planned economy. While consumers (the students) illustrate the importance and need for goods, the government (students from the Office of Prices) decides what will be made, how it will be made, and who receives the product. The end result was often either a surplus of goods and materials not desired or not enough of any given product. In this case, most likely the government members decided to purchase more candy because this sold, while pencils received little attention. Thus, in effect, candy was produced in large numbers based on the *perceived demand* for the product, while pencils showed little demand in the past.

Use the following class money during your simulation.

A Central Planned Economy—Persisting Issues Lesson

Directions: One of the biggest accomplishments and headaches for a socialist nation was its centrally planned economy, where all decisions on what and how much of a product was made was decided by central planners in the government. Read the following scenario below. After doing so, answer and discuss the questions that follow.

You are a manager of a large, government-operated cell phone manufacturer. Last year, the government provided you with enough material to make 50,000 standard cell phones. These phones are not the greatest quality and do not provide many extras compared to other phone manufacturers in other countries. You were given enough material based on last year's sales of phones. With these materials, you make two versions of phones. The first "XC" version has limited memory with a poor quality camera. This phone is cheap to build and was very popular last year. The second "XP" version you make is more expensive. It offers more memory, a better camera, and the ability to download and play music. This is a new phone in your country's market. Last month, a government representative informed you to make 40,000 of the "XC" phone and 10,000 of the "XP" phone.

Within a few weeks, both phones arrive at stores throughout your country. Initial sales indicate the lower quality "XC" model isn't selling well. In fact, only 3,000 phones were sold even though your company continues to manufacturer them. On the other hand, the "XP" has almost sold out the predetermined order of 10,000 phones. Due to the rigid organization and control of the factory, production lines cannot be switched to make more of the "XP" phones. The government has allocated enough material to make a total of 50,000 phones and *no* additional materials will be given to your factory. As a result, you continue to build the outdated, poorer quality "XC" phone after your initial order of "XP" phones are produced and sold. Rather than simply shifting production from the unpopular "XC" phones to the more popular and consumer interested "XP" phone, the government makes an unplanned order to import phones of the same quality as the "XP," costing the government millions of dollars. As a result, based on this year's demand for the "XP" phone, the government will have allocated enough material to make 40,000 "XP" phones and 10,000 "XC" phones for next year.

1. Are there any strengths in this plan of manufacturing?
2. Are there any weaknesses in this plan of manufacturing?
3. How often does cell phone technology change?
4. What, if any, problems exist when you base manufacturing on last year's sales?

The Experiment at Central High—Persisting Issues Lesson

Directions: Read the following experiment about Central High School. Decide if this economic model is both practical and effective.

In the spring of last year, the administration and student council at Central High School sought to revise their approach on selling candy and soda in the school's ten vending machines. This approach was done as an experiment. At the end of school last year, it was decided to sell both products using a "top-down" approach. On the first day of the school's opening, all ten vending machines were placed throughout the building.

It was decided to fill each vending machine with specific types of soda and candy. Each vending machine was then assigned to a predetermined location throughout the school. The machine locations and products sold are as follows:

Machine #1 (in lunch room) sells Snickers, Baby Ruth, and Milky Way.
Machine #2 (in lunch room) sells Diet Coke, Coke, and bottled water.
Machine #3 (outside of the gym) sells Doritos.
Machine #4 (outside of the gym) sells Mountain Dew.
Machine #5 (in the science hallway) sells Sprite.
Machine #6 (in the science hallway) sells pretzels.
Machine #7 (in the math hallway) sells Coke and Dr. Pepper.
Machine #8 (in the math hallway) sells Snickers and Starburst.
Machine #9 (in English hallway) sells Reese's Peanut Butter Cups.
Machine #10 (in English hallway) sells Diet Coke and bottled water.

The initial decision on what and how many items were ordered was based on last year's January sales. Within a matter of days, machines 1, 2, and 7 had sold out, while machines 3, 6, and 10 sold very few items and had a surplus of leftover candy and soda. To add to the dilemma, machines were only operational during passing periods, before school, and during lunch. Such timing created difficulty for students who wished to purchase drinks and candy from machines throughout the school. The school administration and student council had already predetermined what and how much candy and soda would be sold in each machine. *Machines with items still unsold remained in each machine until sold.* All new orders were made once a month and decided upon based on each machine's sales. The end result was a surplus of soda, water, and candy in some vending machines while other machines were sold out.

1. What (if any) are the strengths of using this approach of selling candy and soda?
2. What (if any) are the negatives of using this approach of selling candy and soda?
3. What happens if a popular item sells well one month and not in other months? What would happen if used in Central High's selling plan?
4. Is it okay to have empty machines in some hallways and not in others?

The Bedpan Company: Quality versus Quantity—Simulation

Goals: Given a simulation designed to show and provide students with creative insight into production issues often associated with a planned economy, this simulation is designed for students to understand the planned economy's focus on production, quality, and control versus the free market production often associated with capitalism.

Objectives: Given the opportunity, students will be able to:
1. Compare and contrast similarities and differences encountered in the production of products from both a planned and free market economy.
2. Analyze characteristics of a planned economy.
3. Construct products based on characteristics associated with socialism.

Procedure: Teacher
1. The teacher will need the following materials for this simulation
    a. Clear tape
    b. Scissors
    c. Colored markers or pencils
    d. Handouts for planned production companies (communism)
    e. Handouts for free market production companies (capitalism)
    f. Container of water
2. Explain to students that in a planned economy, the government owns all production. Unlike in a capitalist or free market economy that determines production based on a supply and demand, a planned market economy produces a predetermined amount of a product regardless of consumption, loss in price, or how long it remains unsold.
3. Place students into five groups. Two groups will operate as government-owned and -controlled factories. The remaining three groups will operate independently.
4. Students working under the control of the government (planned economy) should only receive the following materials per group:
    a. Black or brown colored pencils or markers
    b. Limited (predetermined) amounts of tape
    c. Limited (predetermined) amounts of scissors
    d. Limited (predetermined) amounts of materials (bedpan cutouts)
    e. Information sheet provided to each planned economy group
5. Provide all of the above materials to the two government-owned companies. You, the teacher, will act as the government, setting an unrealistic quota of bedpans in a predetermined amount of time. It is recommended that the time requires students to perform under pressure with the predetermined supply of materials. Often, students will find the predetermined goal of production accompanied with the limited supply

of resources (paper, markers, tape, and scissors) manufacturing reliable and quality products are difficult to maintain.
6. Students working under limited government control (free market economy) should receive the following materials per group:
    a. A variety of colored markers or pencils
    b. One roll of tape
    c. Three pairs of scissors
    d. An ample supply of material (bedpan cut-outs)
    e. Information sheet provided for each free market economy group
7. Provide all of the above materials to the three privately owned companies. You, the teacher, will act as the regional wholesale distributor, setting the amount of material provided based on each companies output and sales. It is recommended that the time requires students to perform under pressure with their supply of materials. Often, students will find that producing quality products (bedpans) is more important than mere quantity.
8. Allow all groups to manufacture bedpans for _____ minutes. Monitor all groups.
9. After the given length of time, stop the manufacturing of bedpans. Ask for one representative from each company to discuss their product, how it was made, and the selling price. To ensure the quality of their product, ask for one member of each group to place their bedpan above their head. Poor a small amount of water into the bedpan and examine for leaks and overall quality. Please note this is an optional activity.
10. After all groups have presented their products to the class, lead the class in a brief class discussion. You may wish to ask the following questions:
    a. As your group made the bedpans, were there any issues (either good or bad) that your group encountered?
    b. Did your group feel that a quality product was produced?
    c. Based on the class simulation, which products appear most reliable? Why do you think this is the case?
    d. In terms of consumerism, which system appears to be most effective in providing a quality product?
    e. In terms of providing for the basic needs of the population, which system appears to be most effective?

Procedure: Students
1. Provide the students five groups the following documents:
    a. The German Democratic Republic Bedpan Company
    b. The _____ Bedpan Company
    c. The "cut and fold" diagram

The German Democratic Republic Bedpan Company

Your group is a government-owned and -operated bedpan company. You are one of two companies owned by the government to manufacture bedpans. Like in all socialist/communist nations, the government, based on previous years' sales of bedpans, has allocated you _____ pieces of paper to construct your product. The government (your teacher) has determined you must manufacture _____ bedpans. Your bedpans must have the official "Made in the GDR" label and may only have either brown or black coloring. No additional markings besides the national seal and "Made in the GDR" will be placed on your products. At the end of the time given to make your bedpans, you will report on your progress made and the amount of products produced. Below is your template for your bedpans. Do not modify any of your bedpans.

The _____ Bedpan Company

Your company is one of three privately owned companies in the class. The supply and demand of bedpans determines how much you will produce. Since bedpans are popular, you often construct your pans with extra attention. Your local supplier of materials (your teacher) has supplied you with _____ sheets of paper to begin the manufacturing of bedpans. The competition from other companies is a factor. Your bedpans must be of better quality than your competition. You may decorate your bedpans anyway your company wishes. Below is the template for your bedpans.

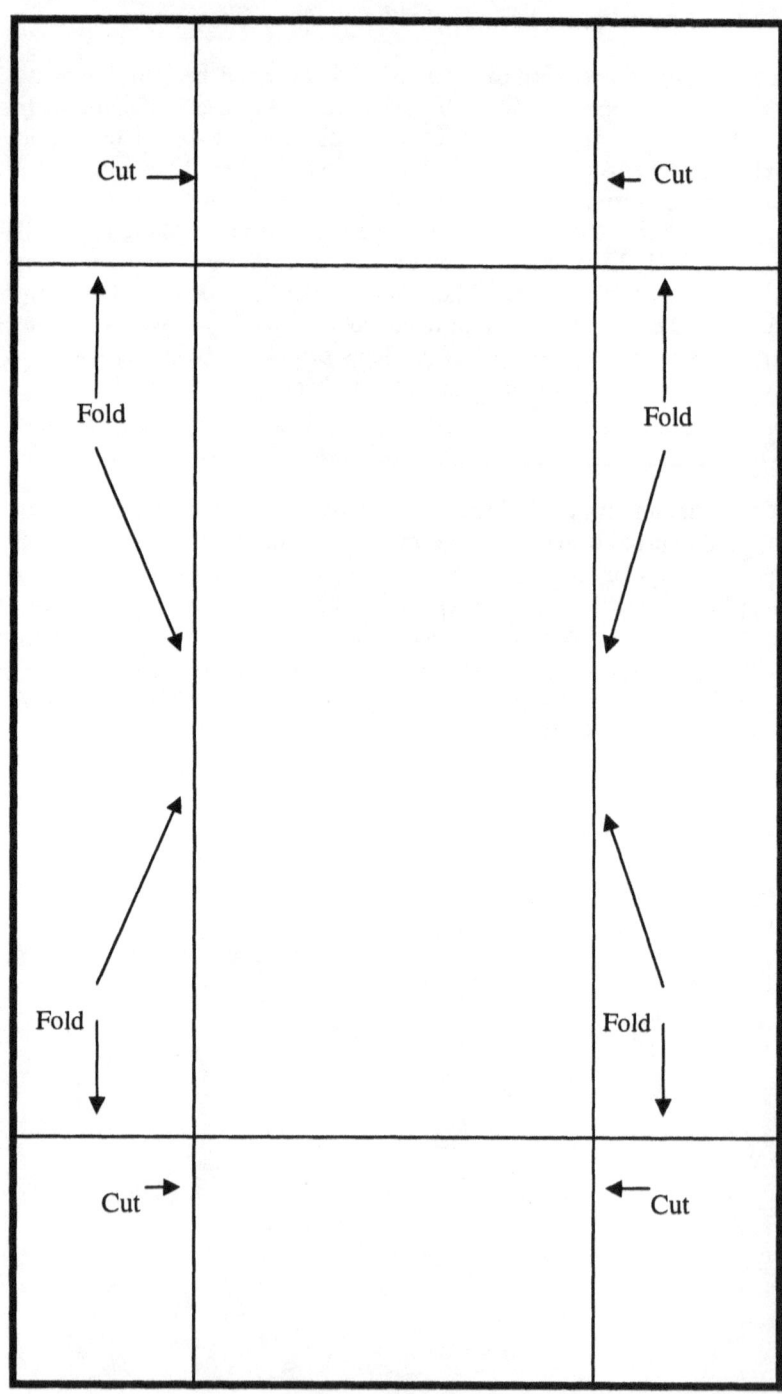

SEVEN

LIFE AND SOCIETY IN EAST GERMANY

SOCIETY AND CULTURE AND THE COMMUNIST GOVERNMENT

From its conception after World War II, it was the goal of the Socialist Unity Party (SED) of East Germany to remodel, change, or eliminate all art, literature, film, and music with the aim to create a "socialist national culture" in efforts to support socialism. To do so, the government implemented strict guidelines in all areas of the arts by implementing harsh and sometimes unrealistic licensing procedures, required by the government, for any notable works to be displayed, illustrated, or performed. Such restrictions followed "liberal phases" of government rule, where rules and regulations often changed with the political elections of members into the SED.

The Ministry for State Security (MfS) or Stasi were tasked to safeguard the SED's cultural policy by using its influence and abilities to maintain both surveillance and control of the population. The MfS unit in charge of security in the areas of culture and general mass communications was the Cultural Association of the GDR. The Cultural Association's mission was to infiltrate and monitor all artists' professional associations, art colleges, art centers, radio and television, movie production, newspapers, theaters, music, and publishers. The underground cultural scene, known as the "hotbed of decadence" and consisting of self-publishers, free artists, writers, singers, and alternative music artists (not authorized by the SED), was actively investigated and undermined through unofficial informers (IMs) and psychological demoralization. In spite of such measures, the underground cultural movement continued to grow (Byg 1990).

SPORTS

East Germany considered itself a sporting nation. The SED believed that by caring about the overall health of its citizens and athletes, the country could receive international success and recognition, in effect making the citizens proud of their country. The Security Area Sport was a division of the MfS. Stasi agents monitored sports in East Germany because it feared "foreign hostile influences" from Western nations and because the MfS had a mistrust of male and female athletes. This monitoring of athletes applied particularly to competitive sports with international ties. In efforts to prevent escape from abroad, Stasi agents limited or denied access with anyone from the West. With the importance placed on sports, performance-enhancing drugs such as Oral-Turinabol were administered in large quantities to children (disguised as vitamin pills) and athletes. Great attention was given by the MfS to ensure "doping" was kept secret. Stasi agents, in additional to their strict surveillance of Olympic sports, created the German College for Physical Education and Sports Medical Service, which over a period of two decades produced some of the world's best athletes (see Table 7.1).

Table 7.1 Olympic Medal Rankings of the German Democratic Republic

Summer Games

Year	City	Gold	Silver	Bronze	Rank
1968	Mexico	9	9	9	5
1972	Munich	20	23	23	3
1976	Montreal	40	25	25	2
1980	Moscow	47	37	42	2
1984	Los Angeles	(boycotted by the GDR)			
1988	Seoul	37	35	30	2

Winter Games:

Year	City	Gold	Silver	Bronze	Rank
1968	Grenoble	1	2	2	10
1972	Sapporo	4	3	7	2
1976	Innsbruck	7	5	7	2
1980	Lake Placid	9	7	7	2
1984	Sarajevo	9	9	6	1
1988	Calgary	9	10	6	2

Source: Rückel 2008.

TRAVEL AND VACATION

In East Germany, the organization or family trips, vacations, and overall leisure was controlled by the government. The official East German travel agency (Reisebüro der DDR) and Young Tourist (Jugendtourist) were the responsible organizations for filing travel plans and making reservations with the exception of State companies and holiday services operated under the direction of the Free German Federation of Trade Unions (FDGB), which allocated employee vacation homes. For the average East German, a typical summer vacation planning process began in February when a worker (vacation candidate) filled out an application at the official vacation agency of their employer (almost always the FDGB), where they requested the vacation spot and country of travel. Before the construction of the Berlin Wall, it was possible to receive limited travel to the West. However, after the Wall was erected in 1961, travel, for the most part, became restricted to Eastern Bloc countries and East Germany itself (see Table 7.2). Even with limited travel to its fellow communist countries, the SED was nervous. Both the East German vacation planners and East German vacationers could make contact with tourists and encourage possible escape. For this reason, the MfS ensured that all tourist and vacation traffic was monitored and kept under close surveillance by the Stasi. Agents from the Office on Special Assignments were deployed in the administration buildings of State travel agencies. Using insider information on applicants, vacation destinations, and countries of travel, Stasi agents built a dense network of IMs among the tour guides to provide helpful information on East German people's contact with West and suspicious individuals (Sheffer 2011).

Table 7.2 Common Travel Destinations for East German Citizens

Trips Arranged by the East German State Travel Agency, 1988

Country	East German Visitors
Czechoslovakia	651,630
Soviet Union	228,304
Hungary	109,637
Bulgaria	63,548
Poland	40,462
Yugoslavia	4,193
Cuba	1,283
Finland (non-communist)	1,010

Source: Rűckel 2008.

Those families that failed to receive reservations to the small number of dream locations along the Baltic Sea often packed up their cars and tents to spend their vacation at a camp site along the northern coast or at the lake. Such "unofficial" accommodations were somewhat political. The government frowned on those who did not use official government lodging, cafeterias, and facilities. Furthermore, such activities by East German citizens limited observational powers of Stasi agents assigned to the Office on Special Assignments.

As a small, personal escape from a structured governmental society, many East Germans chose to "skinny dip" when the opportunity presented itself. The practice of nudism became a mass movement among East Germans. In fact, four in five East Germans indicated they had been skinny dipping at least once, while one in every ten East Germans regularly practiced nudism as a form of expression. Such a response for this popular form of expression was less about sexual freedom and more to do with resisting the external control placed on East Germans by the Government and an opportunity to express a true sign of classlessness (Rückel 2008).

LEISURE

According to the Government, all East Germans were to spend their leisure time in a useful and meaningful way. This meant that citizens were to work as a group or collectively in the community gardens, leisure centers, youth clubs and organizations, or sporting events. In reality, this wasn't the case. While the communist government *believed* its citizens worked tirelessly at a better society during the weekends, most East Germans, by the weekend, were simply tired of the ideological propaganda. The most popular retreat from society itself was the home and the consumption of stimulants. On average, both men and women consumed 286 bottles of beer and 23 bottles of liquor each year (Rückel 2008). It was estimated by the East German government that its citizens consumed more stimulants than any other communist country behind the Iron Curtain. Such consumption illustrated a steady increase in beer, wine, spirits, and cigarettes over thirty-year period (see Table 7.3)

Table 7.3 Consumption of Selected Stimulates per East German (1960-1988)

	Beer (liters)	Wine (liters)	Spirits (liters)	Cigarettes (individual)
1960	80	2.2	4	1,100
1970	92	2.9	5.3	1,300
1980	124	4.1	13	1,700
1988	126	4.3	16	1,900

Source: Rückel 2008.

While there was always a possibility that the Stasi had wired one's apartment, watching Western television was extremely popular. Such practices of watching "Western influences" were frowned upon by the Government. Unofficial informers and Young Pioneers were encouraged by the Stasi to report parents, neighbors, and relatives who received and watched such illegal programming (Funder 2003; Pence and Betts 2011; Fulbrook 2005; Burnett 2007). Because of this continual chance of arrest, many slipped away into their own little world via their dacha (a home-built weekend home). These weekend homes were built through hard work and creativity. Such construction provided an all-important outlet of both creativity and, most importantly, a sense of ownership. While the government wasn't happy about citizens escaping to their private homes and small gardens, they reluctantly conceived that it was better than attempting to escape to the West. Thus, it was considered a "tolerated" luxury.

THE CHURCH

Churches and religious communities in East Germany were considered a thorn in Communist party's side. Since churches in the GDR had a certain amount of independence, they, in return, could give meaning to life and provide hope to the citizens of East Germany. While the Protestant Church was viewed as a threat to the government, the communist government grudgingly developed a liberal approach towards both the Protestant and Lutheran faiths because (1) both Communists and Christians suffered in concentration camps at the hands of Hitler; (2) East Germany was the only Eastern Bloc nation that had a large Protestant Christian population, which allowed for more flexibility compared to the Catholic Church; and (3) the East German government sought to improve relations and acceptance from West Germany. Fair and proper treatment of the Protestant and Lutheran Churches would aid in this acceptance (Baum 1996).

Despite the perceived steps of flexibility for the Church, East German Christians continued to suffer at the hands of the socialist government. Beginning in the 1950s and onward, the communist government began a slow, methodical campaign against Christianity. It did so by: (1) requiring atheist teachings in all public school curriculum based solely on the accomplishments of man; (2) instituting the Jugendweihe or the youth dedication ritual marking the membership into the Socialist party; (3) the government moving to a "rewards and punishment" system against the Church to limit it powers of extracurricular activities such as outdoor festivals, organized sports, and camps to limit its presence; (4) Stasi agents and IMs, working through the Office on Special Assignment, keeping secret files on young Christians who rejected the official government policies. Such rejection of the Jugendweihe ceremony, membership in the Free Germany Youth and others led to the prevention of higher education, quality jobs, and often social acceptance; (5) attempting to influence (through Stasi and IMs) internal dilemmas (e.g., rumors, embezzlement) within given churches to sow mistrust in among followers; and (6) infiltrating religious universities to recruit IMs at the college level to provide detailed information within the Church (Baum 1996; Fulbrook 2005; Diefendorf 1982).

LESSON AND ACTIVITIES

The following lesson is designed to reinforce materials found in this chapter in partnership with the school-adopted content textbook. The following lesson should be used as supplemental text and lesson in an effort to increase cognition over issues associated with life and society in East Germany. Lesson One, "Operation Power Play: East Germany's Policy of the Protestant Church," is a classification lesson that provides students with a detailed view of the East Germans' approach to religion.

Operation Power Play: East Germany's Policy of the Protestant Church—Classification Lesson

Your Dilemma: The date is 17 November 1987. You are a member of the Office on Special Assignments (Stasi, secret police) and assigned to closely monitor churches and religious communities in the GDR. In the past two years, churches throughout the GDR have increased their influence in local towns through actively criticizing government policy and maintaining a safe harbor for environmental, peace, and human rights groups. Such groups and activities are deemed as "subversive" in nature and should be stopped. In addition, the Church is considered an active threat to the GDR because the Church is viewed by a growing portion of the population (1) as a strength in retreat (daily living) for East Germans, (2) for belief in an afterlife, (3) for its ability to connect with the masses through outside activities not connected to Church operations, and (4) because it provides a competing set of values other than communism. Therefore, the government policy (and your mission as a member of the secret police) toward these groups is aimed to stop or at least decrease their influences by means of open or silent repression in the name of national security. Therefore, your possible options/actions are as follows:

A. Infiltrate church seminaries (schools) to recruit IMs to provide future information on both fellow clergy and members.

B. Begin a campaign to squeeze out any form of religious education in schools and increase the pressure to conform to government policy through school-based campaigns.

C. Pressure younger generations to become more active in government-led activities (e.g., Free German Youth) and over time (years), the process of withering away Church support will drop to acceptable levels.

D. Create differences between East German youth and older generations on their views of the Church (e.g., how the Church should be run).

E. Spread misinformation (lies) about pastors from various churches in efforts to effectively turn them against each other and Church policy.

F. Pressure pastors to become politically loyal to the socialist cause and in return, they will receive concessions (breaks) to define the Church cause and directions.

G. Use blackmail (false information) to pressure selected pastors to stepdown.

H. Block acceptance to higher education or expel students who either are not active in the Free German Youth (club for young socialists) or dedicated Socialist party members.

I. Require all youth to be confirmed (accepted) into the *Jugendweihe* (socialist ceremony), representing loyalty to the socialist government.

J. Encourage sport, youth, and family activities on days and times (e.g., Sunday, Wednesday evening) that directly compete with church activities.

K. Limit (through activity permits) the Church's ability to hold outdoor activities, festivals, meetings, or services in efforts to either maintain or eliminate recruiting or membership.
L. Place listening devices (bugs) throughout the targeted church to gather, analyze, and use information against its members.

Instead of trying to implement all of the above options, you believe that some actions have a better chance of success than others. Knowing the potential for success and failure, you must pick the one best options to weaken the Church.

The most realistic option/action to limit the power and influence of the Church is:
1.

Three other options/actions that might work (according to your ranking) are:
2.
3.
4.

The remaining five options/actions that are least likely to work (according to your ranking) are:
5.
6.
7.
8.
9.

Discussion Starters:
1. Which two proposed actions do you believe are most effective in decreasing the growing Church influence? Why?
2. Which two proposed actions do you believe to be most unrealistic and least effective in controlling the Church's influence?
3. When, if ever, does the government have the right to control or influence organizations that directly influence its citizens? Are there exceptions?
4. Of the potential concerns expressed by the East German government about Church threats, which do you believe is most harmful? Least harmful?

EIGHT
THE FALL OF EAST GERMANY

THE BEGINNING OF THE END

The beginning of the Socialist Unity Party's (SED's) fall from power within the Eastern Bloc of communist nations essentially began in the early 1980s. When the East German government experienced a harsh financial crisis in 1982 and 1983, a resulting decrease in both political and military budgets led to decreases in manpower. The recruiting and hiring of Ministry for State Security (MfS) agents was dramatically affected and strained, leaving the ruling government particularly vulnerable to the growing wave of anticommunism developing behind the Iron Wall. Such reductions led to a general decrease in domestic surveillance and internal operations against East German citizens. Accompanying a reduced operational budget, the SED faced increasing resentment from its citizens. In reality, during the 1980s, political resentment in all of the Eastern Bloc countries began to ferment. Criticisms of the Communist party in Hungary and Poland became louder with increased organized political organization against political oppression. In East Germany, the communist leaders simply ignored the growing signals of political upheaval in their neighboring countries. In East Germany, the same men and women remained in power in the government (Schönsee and Lederer 1991). Such political leaders viewed political demonstrations unlikely, but in the instance that an event would occur, the Communist party considered minor, superficial changes rather than the need for political reform. This mentality toward control proved specifically to be the government's downfall. Without the political, military, and economic support from the Soviet Union from 1986 onward, East German leadership regressed into a self-defeating state of denial. The following timeline is designed to highlight the slow destruction of the German Democratic Republic (GDR) from 1980 to 1990.

CHRONICLE TIMELINE

13 October 1980: Due to economic hardships, the East German government increases the minimum required exchange rate for West Berliners visiting relatives in East Berlin in efforts to gain revenue. Such action results in a dramatic drop of visitors entering the GDR and fails to generate substantial revenue for the government.

30 October 1980: Due to increased antigovernment protests in communist Poland and the fear of such actions taking place in East Germany, the visa-free vacation traffic between East Germany and Poland is suspended. This was one of several measures in the SED's attempt at isolation within the Eastern Bloc.

11-13 December 1981: West German Chancellor (president) Helmut Schmidt travels to East Germany for working meetings with East German leader Erich Honecker in efforts to establish better working relations between the two countries. Financial aid is discussed.

13 December 1981: In attempts to stop the growing anticommunist opposition movement and gain control, Poland declares martial law throughout the country. Communist countries within the Eastern Bloc are increasingly concerned with the growing anticommunist movement.

25 January 1982: Based on the growing peace movement within the East German Protestant Church, pastor Rainer Epplemann published the article "Berlin Appeal—Create Peace without Weapons." Stasi agents quickly arrest and detain Epplemann for a brief period of time. The East German government reconsiders its lenient position on the Church.

14 February 1982: The Church of the Cross, located in Dresden (southeastern East Germany), sponsors a peace forum of independent peace groups. The East German government is critical of sponsorship.

25 March 1982: The East German government passes a new border law that increases modifications along the Berlin Wall to make such defenses "more physically challenging" for escape.

1 September 1982: An East German is arrested at a solidarity (free Polish labor union) demonstration in Jena (located in the southern part of East Germany). Government begins to closely monitor all civilian activities.

1 October 1982: West Germany elects a new Chancellor (president), Helmut Kohl.

29 June 1983: The West German government guarantees East Germany a one billion Deutsche Mark to keep the country from bankruptcy.

1 July 1983: The East German government, concerned with growing issues in Poland and Hungary and increased escape attempts of East German citizens, elects to make "further engineering" improvements to the border installations and Berlin Wall to include the controversial automatic firing machine guns along the interior fences.

6 October 1983: Believed to be pressured by the West German government, East German leader Erich Honecker announces the complete dismantling of all automatic firing machine guns along interior fences.

6 April 1984: Thirty-five East Germans, while on vacation in Czechoslovakia, seek refuge in the West German embassy in Prague for five weeks. They return to East Germany with the promise of a fast departure to West Germany. The incident causes panic among high ranking SED members fearing a widespread exodus of citizens.

31 December 1984: The East German government decides to allow nearly 41,000 applicants a departure to West Berlin. Doing so, it was thought, would alleviate the growing resentment towards the communist government and rid the country of trouble-makers.

10 March 1985: Soviet leader Mikhail Gorbachev is elected as the State and Party leader of the Communist party. Considered a reformist, he fosters a sense of autonomy within Eastern Bloc nations.

19-21 November 1985: Soviet leader Mikhail Gorbachev and United States President Ronald Reagan meet in Geneva, Switzerland, to discuss economic, political, and military issues. Both pledge a beginning of "openness."

17-21 April 1986: During the 11th SED's Congress, guest Soviet leader Mikhail Gorbachev asks his fellow East German communists to reflect on party policies through "self-criticism." As a result, East German leadership becomes more and more isolated with politics within the Eastern Bloc.

10 April 1987: Building on the previous year's challenge by the Soviet Union for "self-criticism," a leading East German SED suggests that Gorbachev's vision of *perestroika* is "simply a change of scenery the GDR does not have to participate in or imitate." Such beliefs confirm the government's approach of isolationism with its communist neighbors.

8 June 1987: During a rock concert near the Brandenburg Gate in East Berlin, a riot breaks out between youth and East German police. Such an event illustrated the youth's willingness to openly clash and criticize the government.

5-6 September 1987: The East German government "tolerates" the first unofficial protest by various peace groups in East Berlin. Such actions are viewed by activists as a potential opening or break in strict communist policy.

24-25 November 1987: An East Berlin church is searched by Stasi agents for antigovernment protests. Seven members of the church are arrested and released after protest from church members. After this incident, Stasi and East German police begin selected operations against opposition groups throughout East Germany.

13 February 1988: In the southeastern city of Dresden, Stasi agents and police arrest demonstrators who demand the observance of human rights in East Germany. The protest is quickly controlled by government officials.

18 November 1988: The popular Russian/East German magazine "Sputnik" is pulled from the newsstands after printing an article critical of the SED's beliefs about communism. The "isolation effect" of East Germany continues by banning Soviet anti-Stalinist films.

6 February 1989: Chris Gueffroy, 20 years of age, is the last person shot while attempting to escape to West Berlin.

3 April 1989: The long-standing order to "shoot to kill" along the Berlin Wall is suspended.

2 May 1989: The country of Hungary begins to dismantle its defensive barriers and walls along the Austrian border. This is the first Eastern Bloc country to do so.

7 May 1989: Civil rights protestors in East Germany prove that the communist government has tampered with local elections throughout the country.

July 1989: East Germans begin escaping to Western Europe via Hungary.

30 September 1989: After a week of riots in Leipzig, 5,500 East German citizens overwhelm the Czechoslovakian embassy in search of freedom.

3 October 1989: Travel to Czechoslovakia is terminated in efforts to halt the departure of East Germans to the West.

7-8 October 1989: East German police and Stasi clash with East German protestors in demonstrations against the celebration of the 40th anniversary of the GDR.

9 October 1989: Upward of 70,000 protestors march in the streets of Leipzig. Protestors demand the end of Communist party rule. This was considered one of the largest protests to date against the communist government.

17-18 October 1989: Amid growing pressure from both the SED and citizens, Erich Honecker resigns as Party Chairman. The following day, Egon Krenz is elected Chairman.

21 October 1989: The MfS is directed to "commit itself to change" by the Central Committee.

27 October 1989: The ban on vacation travel to Czechoslovakia is lifted. Thousands flee to the West via Czechoslovakia. Amnesty is granted to all those who have fled East Germany, effectively inviting further departure.

4 November 1989: Over 500,000 demonstrate in East Berlin.

6 November 1989: The order is given for all MfS offices to destroy all material that may be deemed controversial to the government.

7-8 November 1989: The East German government resigns.

9-10 November 1989: East Germans begin to cross the border into West Berlin.

4-5 December 1989: East Germans storm area and district Stasi offices in the fear records and evidence will be destroyed for future prosecutions.

23 February 1990: The East German army is disbanded.

18 March 1990: Free elections in East Germany usher in a resolution to merge with West Germany to become a united Germany.

3 October 1990: The GDR is dissolved.

DETERMINING RESPONSIBILITY

After the official end of the GDR in 1990, the arduous task of determining the responsibility for the crimes that took place along the Berlin Wall began. Since most of the alleged crimes against East Germany involved the Berlin Wall, such a location became the top priority of German courts. In all, 230 East Germans were killed trying to escape East Berlin, with another 900 wounded by the communist regime (Flemming 2009). Beginning in 1990, German courts began to investigate cases associated with the Berlin Wall. The difficult task of investigating, locating witnesses, and determining personal fault was often ambiguous. Was the border guard who was ordered to shoot responsible for the death of a fellow East German? Was the commanding officer in charge of the border guards responsible for giving the orders? Or were the members of the Communist party who funded and built the wall responsible for the oppression of its people? Due to an agreement with West Germany before unification, it was determined that no trials of East German officials would take place unless such officials broke laws within the GDR before reunification. Within a nine-year period (1990-1999), seventy trials of border guards, politicians, and military officers took place. Charges of "attempted or successful manslaughter" were determined unlawful under the East German constitution (McAdams 2005; Quint 2000), which successfully paved the way for prosecution of former East German officials and border guards. While most border guards were convicted of manslaughter and received suspended sentences, politicians did not fare as well (see Table 8.1). Due to the influence of communist members in the Politburo and MfS on making important decisions for the country, convicted prison sentences averaged six years for being "direct perpetrators" for fatal shots at the Berlin Wall (Flemming 2009; Burnett 2007). The last sentence was handed out in 1999.

Table 8.1 Example of High Profile Trials of Former East German Officials

Name	**Government Position**	**Trial/Sentence**
Erich Honecker	Chairman of East Germany	Stopped due to health
Erich Mielke	Leader of State Security	Stopped due to health
Willi Stoph	Prime Minister	Stopped due to health
Heinz Keßler	Defense Minister	Guilty, 5-7 years
Fritz Streletz	Deputy Defense Minister	Guilty, 5-7 years
Klaus Baumagarten	Border Troop Commander	Guilty, 6 years
Egon Krenz	Politburo Member	Guilty, 6 years

Source: Flemming 2009.

LESSON AND ACTIVITIES

The following lesson is designed to reinforce materials found in this chapter in partnership with the school-adopted content textbook. The following lesson should be used as supplemental text and lessons in an effort to increase cognition over issues associated with eventual fall of the GDR and the legal issue of crimes committed along the Berlin Wall. Lesson One, "Accountability for Wall Shootings," is a persisting issues lesson that provides students with an idea of accountability for both border guards and commanding officers after the fall of the Wall.

Accountability for Wall Shootings—Persisting Issues Lesson

Directions: Read the following paragraphs then answer the questions below.

Jűrgen Schmidt was a twenty-one-year-old border guard assigned to Alpha Detachment along the Berlin Wall near Potsdamer Platz. This was Jűrgen's second month into his mandatory military service. In the last few months, potential escapees have been shot while trying to escape to West Berlin by different border guard detachments along the Wall. While most escape attempts took place during the early morning hours, Jűrgen's commanding officer informed his men that it was only "a matter of time before traitors attempted to escape West in their sector of the Wall." Indeed, the commanding officer was correct. Suspicious activity had been reported in Jűrgen's sector of the Wall. Increased patrols indicated no activity, but the possibility of detaining an escapee was always real. In the past, the standing order for all border guards was "shoot to kill." Naturally, some guards, as tough as they might act, didn't have the stomach to kill a fellow East German. Indeed, after brief discussions with his fellow guards, nobody wanted to take a human life unless absolutely necessary.

On the evening of 22 October 1983 while on a motorized motorcycle patrol, Jűrgen noticed two middle-aged men climbing the first barrier (fence). Not being able to make direct contact with the two men, Jűrgen attempted to ride to their position as fast as he could. Having been spotted, the men began their escape past the observation tower. Jűrgen radioed for assistance, but no support replied. He feared that his fellow border guards might have been hurt or killed by the men. In haste, he attempted to contact his commanding officer. In frustration, he was unable to reach any superior officer. Jűrgen was in a dilemma. If he allowed the two men to escape, he would likely be imprisoned; if he captured them, he could be a hero in the eyes of the government; if he killed them, he would have such guilt for years to come. As he yelled for the two men to stop, he pulled his automatic rifle from his back. Seeing the men within sites of his weapon, he fired a warning shot. Both men continued to run. Now, Jűrgen wasn't sure what to do

Questions:

1. What would you probably do if you were Jürgen's situation?
2. Would Jürgen have the authority to shoot both men in this situation? Why? Why not?
3. If you received orders from your superiors to kill the escapees but you didn't, should this be grounds for court martial trial?
4. Would your decision for questions 1-3 change if you learned that the two men attempting to escape knew government secrets that could harm your country if leaked to the West Germany?
5. If you shot and killed the two men, should your commander be held accountable in the years after the Wall came down? Why or why not?
6. Should an individual who follows orders be held accountable after the fact?

REFERENCES

Baum, Gregory. *The Church for Others: Protestant Theology in Communist East Germany.* Grand Rapids: William B. Eerdmans Publishing Company, 1996.
Bonwell, Charles C., and James A. Eison,. *Active Learning: Creating Excitement in the Classrooms*, Washington D.C. Eric Clearinghouse on Higher Education (ERIC Document Reproduction No. ED340272, 1991).
Burnett, Simon. *Ghost Strasse: Germany's East Trapped between Past and Present.* Montreal: Black Rose Books, 2007.
Byford, Jeffrey, and W. B. Russell. 2006. Analyzing public issues—Clarification through discussion: A case study of social studies teachers. *Social Studies Review* 46 (1): 70–72.
Byg, Barton. 1990. Cinema in the German Democratic Republic. *Monatshefte* 82 (3):286–293.
Chiodo, John J., and J. Byford. 2004. Do they really dislike social studies? A study of middle school and high school students. *The Journal of Social Studies Research* 28 (1):16–26.
Diefendorf, Jeffry. 1982. Teaching history in the polytechnical school of the German Democratic Republic. *The History Teacher* 15 (3):347–361.
Driscoll, Marcy P. *Psychology of Learning for Instruction*, 3rd ed. Boston, MA: Allyn & Bacon Press, 2005.
Flemming, Thomas. *The Berlin Wall: Division of a City.* Landshut: Bosch Druck Publishers, 2009.
Fritz, Oliver. *The Iron Curtain Kid.* Lexington, KY: Self publication, 2009.
Fulbrook, Mary. *Anatomy of a Dictatorship: Inside the GDR 1949-1989.* Oxford: Oxford University Press, 1997.
Fulbrook, Mary. *The People's State: East German Society from Hitler to Honecker.* New Haven: Yale University Press, 2005.
Funder, Anna. *Stasiland: Stories from Behind the Berlin Wall.* London: Gran Books, 2003.
Hansel, Jana. *After the Wall: Confessions from an East German Childhood and the Life that came Next.* New York: Public Affairs Publishing, 2004.
Hoagland, Matthew A. *Utilizing Constructivism in the History Classroom.* Bloomington, IN. Eric Clearinghouse for Higher Education (ERIC Document Reproduction No. ED482436, 2009).
Gieseke, Jens. *The GDR State Security: Shield and Sword of the Party.* Berlin: The Federal Commission for the Records of the State Security Service of the Former German Democratic Republic, 2006.
Jeffries, Ian, and M. Melzer. *The East German Economy.* London, UK: Croom-Helm Publishers, 1987.
Krathwohl, David R. 2002. A revision of Bloom's taxonomy: An overview. *Theory into Practice* 41 (4):212–218.

Krieger, Larry. *World History: Perspectives on the Past*. San Diego: Houghton Mifflin, Hardcourt Publishing, 1994.
Koehler, John O. *Stasi: The Untold Story of the East German Secret Police*. Boulder, CO: Westview Press, 1999.
Kunselman, Julia, and K. Johnson. 2004. Using the case study method to facilitate learning, *College Teaching* 52 (3):87–92.
Lottich, Kenneth. 1963. Extracurricular indoctrination in East Germany. *Comparative Educational Review* 6 (3):209–211.
McAdams, James. 2005. The Honecker trial: The East German past and the German future. *The Review of Politics* 58 (1):75–152.
Mills, Carol J., and W. G. Durden. 1992. Cooperative learning and ability grouping: An issue of choice. *Gifted Child Quarterly* 36 (1):11–16.
Nolan, John, and J. Byford. 2004. Escape from Berlin. *Southern Social Studies Journal* 29 (2):52–71.
Pence, Katherine, and P. Betts. *Socialist Modern: East German Everyday Culture and Politics*. Ann Arbor: University of Michigan Press, 2011.
Quint, Peter. 2000. The Border Trials and the East German Past–Seven Arguments. *The American Journal of Comparative Law* 58 (4):541–572.
Rūckel, Robert. *The GDR Guide: Everyday Life in a Long Gone State in 22 Chapters*. Berlin: Druckhaus Publishing, 2008.
Russell, William, and J. Byford. 2006. The evolution of man and his tools: A simulation from the MACOS project. *The Journal for the Liberal Arts and Sciences*, 10 (3):17–21.
Schönsee, Reinhert, and G. Lederer. 1991. The gentle revolution. *Political Psychology* 12 (2):309–330.
Sheffer, Edith. *Burned Bridge: How East and West Germans Made the Iron Curtain*. New York: Oxford University Press, 2011.
Simonovits, Andras. 1989. Hidden investment cycles in socialist economies. *The Scandinavian Journal of Economics*, 91 (3):583–597.
Stitziel, Judd. *Fashioning Socialism: Clothing, Politics and Consumer Culture in East Germany*. Oxford: Berg Press, 2007.
Slavin, Robert E. *A Practical Guide to Cooperative Learning*. Boston: Allyn & Bacon Press, 1994.
Stahl, Robert J. 1979. Working with values and moral issues in content-centered science classrooms. *Science Education* 63 (2):183–194.
Turner, Henry. *The Two Germanies since 1945*. New Haven: Yale University Press, 1987.
VanSledright, Bruce A. 2004. What Does it mean to Think Historically . . . and How do you Teach It?" *Social Education* 68 (3):230–233.
Watts, Michael. 1994. Was There Anything Left of the "Socialist Personality" Values of Eastern and Western German youth at the beginning of unification. *Political Psychology* 15 (3):215–232.
Wheeler, Sarah. 2006. Role-Playing games/simulations for international issues-courses. *Journal of Political Science Education* 2 (3):331–347.
Zatlin, Jonathan. *The Currency of Socialism: Money and Political Culture in East Germany*. Washington: Cambridge University Press, 2009.

INDEX

Berlin Wall, 64–65, 75

Christianity, campaign against, 101
Case study method, 2, lesson, 48
Central Committee, 32–33, 38
Communist political/economic system, 31–32
Church, 101
Classification format, 14, lesson, 14, 35, 102
Content-centered learning, 8

Escape from Berlin, 64–65, simulation, 69
Espionage operations, 43

Forced-choice format, 8, lessons, 59, 73
Free German Federation of Trade Unions, 98

Grading rubric, 21, 72

Inductive inquiry, 26, lessons, 37, 78

Jugendweihe, 75–76

Mielke, Erich, 29
Military (Volksarmee), 41
Ministry for State Security (Stasi), history, 41, 42, total surveillance, 44

Party Congress, 31–32, 38
Planned economy, 81, 83, 84
Persisting issues, 22, lessons, 40, 46, 57, 61, 91–92, 110
Politburo, 32, 33
Political parties, district and local, 32, elective, 43, opponent labels, 43
Post war transformation of society, 29
Prison, 43–44

Rank-order format, 11, lesson, 66

Secretariat, 38
Simulations, 17, 69, 88, 93
Socialist Unity Party (SED), 30, fall, 104
Society, and the Church, 101, consumption and manufactering, 96, drug use, 100, sports, 97, 98, travel and vacation, 98, 99, youth, 75
Soviet Military Administration (SMA), 29
Stage in becoming a good Socialist, 75
Stasi (Ministry for State Security), history, 41, 42, total surveillance, 44

Timeline of events, 105
Trials of former East German officials, 109, determining responsibility, 108

Unofficial informers (IMs), 42, 65

Volksarmee (military), 41
Volkskammer (East German Parliament), 30

West Berlin Dilemma, 63
West Germany, 44–45
World War II, 29, 81, 99

www.ingramcontent.com/pod-product-compliance
Lightning Source LLC
Chambersburg PA
CBHW031554300426
44111CB00006BA/306